# ACCELERATE

## FOUNDER INSIGHTS INTO ACCELERATOR PROGRAMS

FG PRESS | BOULDER, COLORADO

*Accelerate: Founder Insights Into Accelerator Programs*

Printed in the United States of America.

LAYOUT DESIGN | Kevin Barrett Kane

COVER DESIGN | Jack Dillé

ILLUSTRATIONS | James P. Carter

PRIMARY TYPEFACES | Gotham and Helvetica Neue

# FG PRESS
PUBLISHED BY | FG Press
Boulder, Colorado
fgpress.com

# ACCELERATE

## FOUNDER INSIGHTS INTO ACCELERATOR PROGRAMS

WRITTEN BY
## LUKE DEERING

CO-WRITTEN BY
## MATT CARTAGENA &
## CHRIS DOWDESWELL

FOREWORD BY
## BRAD FELD

CO-CREATED BY
## AN AMAZING GROUP OF
## OVER 150 ENTREPRENEURS

# CO-CREATED BY:

Ben Congleton – Co-founder & CEO, Olark; Rickey Yean – Co-founder & CEO, Crowdbooster; Kathryn Minshew – Co-founder & CEO, The Daily Muse; Pete Koomen and Dan Siroker – Co-founders, Optimizely; James Fong – Co-founder & CEO, Listia; Ben Lerner – CEO, DataNitro; Wojciech Gryc – Co-founder & CEO, Canopy Labs; Yu-Kuan Lin – Co-founder, Everyday.me; Carol Roth – media pundit and bestselling author of *The Entrepreneur Equation*; Matt Colyer – Co-founder, Easel; Daniel Palacio – Founder, Authy; Dom Lewis – Co-founder & CEO, Tray.io; Maila Reeves – Director of Strategic Relationships & PR, ProFinda.com; Jakub Nesetri – Co-founder & CEO, Apiary; Melissa Clark-Reynolds – CEO, MiniMonos; David Buxton – Founder, Arachnys; Patrick Elliott – Co-founder, Backscratchers; Alex Depledge – Co-founder, Hassle; Julian Keenaghan – Co-founder, Tastebuds.fm; Nicolai Watzenig – Co-founder & CEO, Birdback; Ev Kontsevoy – Co-founder & CEO, MailGun; Ivo Minjauw – Co-founder & CEO, SocialExpress; Stefano Cutello – Co-founder & CEO, PastBook; Jack Tai – Co-founder & CEO, Notesolution; Jude Ower – Founder, PlayMob; Ajay Meht – Co-founder, FamilyLeaf; Christian Nkurunziza – Co-founder, Tenscores; Aaron Harris – Co-founder & CEO, Tutorspree; Jon Pospischil – Co-founder, Custora; Dave Fowler – Co-founder & CEO, Chartio; Ray Grieselhuber – Co-founder & CEO, Ginzametrics; Mike Turitzin – Co-founder, WorkFlowy; Rod Ebrahimi – Co-founder & CEO, ReadyForZero; Lee Lin – Co-founder, RentHop; Ryan Nielsen – Co-founder, Tumult; Yrjö Ojasaar – Co-founder & CEO, Publification; Seth Priebatsch – Chief Ninja, LevelUp; Danielle Weinblatt – CEO, Take the Interview; Jack Groetzinger – Founder, SeatGeek; Sune Alstrup Johansen – Co-founder & CEO, The Eye Tribe; Oliver Lukesch – Co-founder & CEO, Weavly; Jeremy Easterbrook – Co-founder & CEO, Prestopolis; Mikael Cho – Co-founder & CEO, ooomf; Ankit Gupta – Co-founder, Innovese; Christian Atz – Co-founder, colored.by; Protik Roychowdhury – Co-founder, croak.it; Brett Hellman – CEO, hall; Clark Benson – Founder & CEO, Ranker; Ethan Austin – Founder & CEO, GiveForward; Jose Li – Founder & CEO, 71lbs; David LaBorde – Co-founder, SwiftPayMD; Joe Reger Jr. – Co-founder, Springbot; Howard H. Hamilton – Founder & CEO, Soccermetrics; Pete Moore – Co-founder & CEO, Ninja Blocks; Daniel Noble – Founder, Wooboard; Chris Thür – Co-founder & CEO, Ovelin; Cindy Gallop – Founder, IfWeRanTheWorld; Vanessa Dawson – Founder, Evry; Marci Harris and Rachna Choudhry – Founding Team, POPVOX; Diane Tate – Manager, Mozilla WebFWD accelerator program; Alex Tryon – Founder & CEO, Artsicle; Cheryl Yeoh – Co-founder & CEO, Reclip.It; Laura Fitton – Founder, oneforty, and author of *Twitter for Dummies* and currently Inbound Marketing Evangelist at HubSpot; Jesse Draper – Founder and host, The Valley Girl Show; Jacqueline Dinsmore – Co-founder & CEO, Luvali; Sonia Kapadia – Founder & CEO, Taste Savant; Kellee Khalil – Founder & CEO, Lover.ly; Marianne Sea – Co-founder, Young Republic; Kyle Smitley – Founder & CEO, barley & birch; Juliette Brindak – CEO, Miss O and Friends; Tanya Huang – Founder, Knot Theory; Melissa Gonzalez-Caputo – Founder & CEO, Lion'esque Style; Lynley Sides – Co-founder & CEO, The Glue Network; Mike Abasov – Founder, MBF; Emma Jones – Founder, Enterprise Nation; Celia Gates – Founder, The Observatory; Bradley Joyce – Founder & CEO, Socialyzer; Garrett Gee

– Co-founder, Scan.me; Afifa Siddiqui – Co-founder & CEO, Careerleaf; Hany Rashwan – Founder & CEO, Ribbon; Jaclyn Sharp – Founder, Imposter; Mike Salter – Co-founder & Creative Director, We Are Pop Up; Matthew Waldman – Founder, NOOKA; Jennifer Reuting – Founder & CEO, DocRun; Rogier Trimpe – Co-founder & CEO, VideoView; Cristian Andreica – Co-founder & CEO, Nexi; Miquel Ros – Co-founder, GourmetOrigins; Derek Dodge – Founder, 1Mind; Jindou Lee – Founder, Happy Inspector; Sam Friedman – CEO, and Alex Israel – CEO, ParkMe; Vincenzo Acinapura – Co-founder & technical director, and Simone Pozzobon – Co-founder & CEO, Foooblr; Michele Redolfi – Co-founder & CEO, Moku; Ai Ching Goh – Co-founder, Piktochart; Trevor Koverko – CEO, eProf; Jonathan Jenkins – Founder & CEO, OrderWithMe; Erik Lumer – Founder, CircleMe; Daniel Bailey, Co-founder, Iup, and Founder, ConceptKicks.com; Alex Moore – Founder & CEO, Baydin; Bernie Yoo – Co-founder, Bombfell; Rob Lenderman – Co-founder & CIO, BoostCTR; David Greenbaum – Co-founder & CEO, BoostCTR; Maxine Manafy – Founder & CEO, Bunndle; Khuram Hussain – Co-founder & CEO, Fileboard; Young Han – Co-founder & CEO, GoVoluntr; Manuel Medina – Co-founder & CEO, Grouptalent; Nathan Parcells – Co-founder & CMO, InternMatch; Mike Lewis – President & Co-founder, Kapost; Vitaly Golomb – Founder & CEO, Keenprint; Jason Traff – Co-founder, Leaky; Nick Soman – Founder & CEO, LikeBright; Ken Johnson – Co-founder, Manpacks; Katrina Brickner – Co-founder, Marquee; Wink Jones – Co-founder & CEO, Mealticket; Ryan Stoner – Founder & CEO, MoPix; Alex White – Co-founder & CEO, NextBigSound; Nirav Tolia – Founder & CEO, Nextdoor; Camilo Acosta – Co-founder & CEO, PayByGroup; John De Goes – Founder & CEO, Precog; Reece Pacheco – Founder & CEO, Shelby.tv; Adam Bonnifield – Co-founder, Spinnakr; Justin DeLay – Co-founder, TempoDB; Miro Kazakoff – Co-founder & CEO, Testive; Tom Rose – Co-founder & CPO, Testive; Dave Bisceglia – Co-founder & CEO, The Tap Lab; Steve Krenzel – Co-founder, Thinkfuse; Brandon Bloom – Co-founder, Thinkfuse; Ryan Holiday, bestselling author of *Trust Me I'm Lying* and Director of Marketing at American Apparel; Marc Lizoain – Co-founder & CEO, Urtak; Kieran Farr – Co-founder & CEO, VidCaster; Todd Silverstein – Co-founder & CEO, Vizify; Jay Lee – Co-founder & CEO, Smallknot; Ben Dilts – Co-founder & CEO, Lucidchart; Karl Sun – Co-founder & CTO, Lucidchart; Ilya Sukhar – Co-founder & CEO, Parse; Dana Severson – Founder & CEO, Chasm.io; Dean Fankhauser – CEO, Nuji; Boštjan Špetič – CEO, Zemanta; Kristo Kaarmann – CEO, TransferWise; Gabriel Hubert – CEO;  Stanislas Polu – CEO, Nitrogram and Seedcamp; Mat Elis - Founder, Cloudability; Raj Aggarwal, Henry Cipolla, and Andrew Rollins - Co-founders, Localytics; Kevin Heap, Spencer Smith, and Joe Wilson - Co-founders, Overlay Studio, Inc.; Isaac Saldana, Tim Jenkins, and Jose Lopez - Co-founders, Sendgrid, Carly Gloge, Isaac Squires, and Gavin Lee - Co-founders, Ubooly; Ben Uretsky, Jeff Carr, Moisey Uretsky, Mitch Wainer, and Alec Hartman - Co-founders, Digital Ocean; with introductions by Pat Riley, Executive Director of the Global Accelerator Network, and Alex Iskold, Managing Director of Techstars New York.

# ACKNOWLEDGEMENTS

This book would not have been possible were it not for our incredible supporters who found us through Kickstarter. Thank you so much to:

Charlie Houchin, 2012 US Olympian & Gold Medalist; Cisco; Codlo; David S. Rose; Jason Traff; Brad Feld; Dark Justice; MVPCreator.com; Emma Jones MBE; Julia Macmillan; Walter McLeod; Eco Capital Startups; John Frewin; Daniel Fülep; Christina (Kina) De Santis; Marit Tuominen; Jess Williamson; Michael Polifonte; Rick Allen; Stefano Cutello; Patrick Vlaskovits; DC Cahalane; Jaclyn Sharp; Simon Jenner; BuiltInCork; SoundBoard Angel Fund; Jonathan Hakakian; NewTide Commerce, Inc.; Cynthia Retuerto; Rockstart Accelerator; Samantha Monday; Lezlie Moleiro Dias; Gyllensvaan; Jaclyn Sharp; Matthew P Henry; Dave Bisceglia; Dean Cooney; Sara Shenouda; Gust; Kishan Patel; Suzie H; Kathleen Fritzsche; Startup Stuttgart; Wolfie; Greg Fisher; Theo den Brinker; Steve Krenzel; Matthias Ludwig; Sam Gherman; Bruce Higa-Tahara; Steve Sebestyen; Julien L. Pham, MD, MPH; Magnus Erixzon; Masha Adamian; Tony Schy; Matthew Anderson; SG; Melody Wilding; Marquee; Howard Haines; Rukesh Patel; Michael Weiss; Joseph Austin Sullivan; Daniel Bailey; Southern Swallow; Mozart Venture Partners; Correlation Ventures; Jeff 'SKI' Kinsey; Celia Gates; The Global Brainstorm; Oliver Lukesch; Saroj Ativitavas; mojo; Constantine Ivanov; Stefan Patak; Bogobooks; Felix Cramer von; Clausbruch; Rod Ebrahimi; Samuel Pavin; Andy Fernandez; Tom Denison; Astrid Paramita Mochtarram; Jane Smorodnikova; Christian H. Leeb; eddywebs; Negociando tu salario; Sinead Wilson-Devane; Sinead Mac Manus; VentureSpace Accelerator; Satoru Hirose; Arden Dertat; Jonathan Pollinger; Ajay Yadav; Ross Malaga; Cristian Andreica; Kean Gardner; Nazia Iqbal; Jude Ower; Joel Gascoigne; Tom Holdsworth; Sashka Rothchild; Sune Alstrup Johansen; Andrew Cleland; Dave Fowler; Kieran Lee Farr; Juliettte Brindak; Bernat Fages; Brian Speronello; Ajay Mehta; Per Håkansson; Gaurav Tiwari; Christian W. Atz; Olof von Lindequist; Andrew Kinzer; Max Rostotski; Jonathan Deutsch; Tony Thomas; Chad; Heinz Grünwald; Noemy Jorge; Christian Busch; Benoit Pothier; Brad Wilcox; Jason Malki; Diane Tate; Chris Hawkins; Michael Weider; Will Hichens; laura manistre; John J Pope; Adelina Peltea; Shannon Ley; Alex Hantman; Maxine Manafy; Dhruv Kar; Dominic Savoie; Davide Savazzi; and Valery Komissarova.

A special thank you to our amazing mums for supporting our ideas and putting up with us as entrepreneurs—Elizabeth Deering, Joanne Jobeck, and Sarah Clegg.

We would also like to share a special thank you to Brad Feld, David S. Rose, Joseph Austin Sullivan, Daniel Bailey, and Kean Gardner.

# TABLE OF CONTENTS

# FOREWORD

In 2006 when David Cohen met with me for the first time to tell me about the idea he had for a 'mentor driven accelerator,' neither of us had any idea the concept would turn into a worldwide phenomenon that would help change the way company creation and early stage investing worked.

I was sitting in my office in Boulder having one of my random days. On these days, I spend fifteen minutes with anyone who wants to meet with me. I have an automated calendar set up and do this periodically—at the time I was doing it once a month. It took David about three months to get on my calendar. He was patient—and persistent—key qualities of any entrepreneur.

I didn't know David. We were angel investors in a few companies together so I recognized his name, but had no idea who he was. He sat down across from me and quickly launched into a description of his idea for Techstars. He was frustrated with how angel investing worked and wanted to help start more companies and engage deeply with the entrepreneurs. He was also interested in getting more connected to the Boulder startup community.

David and his partner David Brown had been successful entrepreneurs. They had bootstrapped a company—PinPoint Technologies—and sold it for a small fortune to a public company called Zoll. After working for Zoll for five years, David Cohen was ready to do it again. But he had a bigger idea than just starting one company.

Seven years later, Techstars now has mentor-driven accelerator programs around the US, in Boulder, Boston, New York, Seattle, Austin, and Chicago. In the summer of 2013, its first international program started in London . It has partnered with organizations like Nike and Kaplan to develop mentor-driven accelerators around these companies' brands. And Techstars co-founded the

Global Accelerator Network to help coordinate and share best practices around mentor-driven accelerators around the world.

The accelerator movement has changed how companies get created. It is part of the fabric that ties entrepreneurs, mentors, and investors together in a startup community. It has inspired entrepreneurship all over the world, and reinforces the idea that entrepreneurship is vibrant in many different cities and industries.

Luke and his co-authors have interviewed numerous entrepreneurs and participants in accelerator programs to bring you a view from the inside of how accelerator programs work. It is a great survey of a wide range of experiences, and will give anyone interested in participating in or starting an accelerator a deep understanding of what goes on.

When David and I co-founded Techstars with David Brown and Jared Polis, we had no idea what would or could happen. We just got started, ran an experiment, measured what happened, and iterated on it. Seven years later, Techstars has exceeded our wildest dreams, and the sheer number of mentor-driven accelerators is a phenomenon we never could have envisioned. Luke captures the magic well in *Accelerate* and helps add to the understanding of a new way to create startups.

*Brad Feld*
Boulder, CO

9

# INTROD

UCTION

# INTRODUCTION

This book is a collection of thoughts written by business founders who have graduated from a startup accelerator program. In effect, you could see this book as a startup Q&A session on steroids, and as a guide to the ever-changing landscape of startup accelerators, featuring the experiences and learnings of their graduates. *Accelerate* is designed to help broaden your real-life knowledge base on starting a company, while also giving you a strong foundation from which to accelerate your own entrepreneurial growth through participating in an accelerator program.

The book was co-created by over 150 entrepreneurs who have taken their company through an accelerator program or created an accelerator, along with a sprinkling of entrepreneurs who have not participated in the accelerator program experience. Some American accelerator programs whose graduates are featured in this book are Y Combinator, Techstars, 500 Startups, AngelPad, Launchpad LA, and DreamIt. Internationally we feature startups from programs such as Techstars London (formerly Springboard), StartupBootCamp and RockStart in Amsterdam, Startup Sauna in Finland, FounderFuel in Canada, StartMate in Australia, China Accelerator in Dalian, and iAccelerate in India.

For those that feel an accelerator might be an appropriate method for building your startup, we provide a comprehensive list of 230 accelerator programs, along with a list of the top thirty most successful programs in the world. If you're looking to join an accelerator and don't know where to begin, *Accelerate* provides a wealth of information concerning the inner workings of accelerator programs.

# THE WORLD'S STARTUP ACCELERATOR PROGRAMS

Before jumping into this book, it is important to understand the language being used around an accelerator. Often, the terms "incubator" and "accelerator" are used interchangeably although they are quite different terms at their core. One way to explain these differences is through a simple analogy: incubators can be thought of as startup gyms—equipped with the necessary resources, environment, and guidance to grow your startup—while accelerators can be thought of as startup boot camps—just as equipped as incubators, but involving a more defined mission, application process, methodology for progress, and stakeholders. All in all, accelerators tend to focus more deliberately on achieving certain success criteria for a startup.

Startup accelerators are typically for-profit organizations that foster a physical environment that supports accelerated growth for startups. Programs or cohorts tend to consist of around ten teams who are supported by the accelerator with a small amount of funding, typically averaging $20,000. Some of the top tier accelerators also offer an option where their startups can receive up to $150,000 in additional seed funding. The classes typically run for three months, during which the startups receive mentoring, training, and a chance to increase their network beyond that which they could have achieved organically. The process culminates in Demo Day, where the startups pitch their company to an audience full of investors. In exchange for the services provided by the accelerator, the startups give the accelerator anywhere from 3–25% in equity; however, most accelerators tend to ask for around 6%.

# THE LANDSCAPE OF

# ACCELERATOR

# PROGRAMS

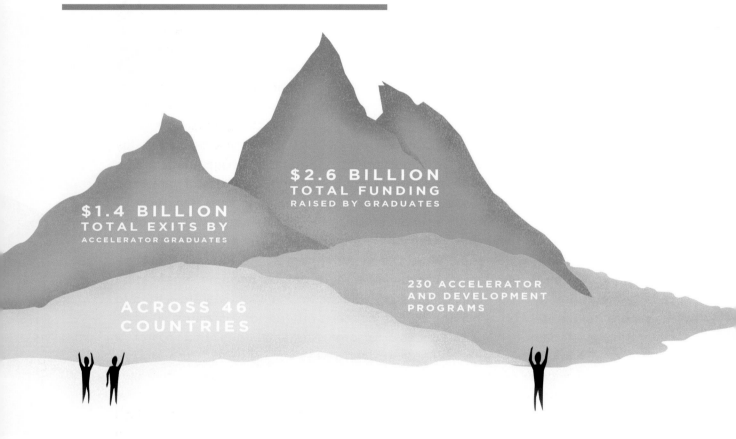

$1.4 BILLION
TOTAL EXITS BY
ACCELERATOR GRADUATES

$2.6 BILLION
TOTAL FUNDING
RAISED BY GRADUATES

230 ACCELERATOR
AND DEVELOPMENT
PROGRAMS

ACROSS 46
COUNTRIES

*For this introduction, we asked Pat Riley, the Executive Director of the Global Accelerator Network, to contribute his thoughts on the landscape of accelerator programs. The Global Accelerator Network consists of over 70 of the top startup accelerators from around the world including Techstars, Flat6Labs, StartupBootcamp, and Launchpad LA. All accelerators in the GAN utilize a mentorship-based, short-term model with terms that are extremely favorable to entrepreneurs. The GAN started alongside the White House's Startup America initiative and continues to provide networking opportunities, training, special perks, and ongoing support for its members and their entrepreneurs. Here's what Pat has to say:*

In the late 1990s numerous incubators appeared all over the world. They initially did a good job bringing together founders in meaningful and effective ways, especially around a physical location. Unfortunately, many of these incubators turned into real estate plays where the incubator owners focused on exploiting short-term gains made by startup entrepreneurs during the fervor around the Internet, mostly in exchange for providing space. Ultimately, many incubators did not solely focus on the long-term successes of these startups and as a result disappeared in the aftermath of the collapse of the Internet bubble.

In 2005, there was a huge dearth of early stage capital and seed capital for new startups, especially for first time entrepreneurs. It's hard to believe that in today's current startup and innovation environment, but the hangover from the Internet bubble was still lingering and VC and angel investors were hesitant to invest in anything.

During this time period, Y Combinator gave birth to the modern day accelerator by creating a model where a modest number of companies go through a time constrained program to help them get their business up and running. In exchange for the program and a small amount of seed funding Y Combinator took a small equity stake in each company. Suddenly, a new model was created that aligned incentives between the startup and the accelerator, providing the startup with focused advice, help, and a small amount of capital, while allocating the some equity upside to the accelerator.

In 2006, Techstars built upon this model by developing the mentorship-driven accelerator, which incorporated a significant number of active mentors into the program. In the first Techstars program, launched in Boulder in 2007, there were over 50 active mentors in the 90 day program, each of whom spent time helping and advising one or more of the companies in the program. This model has continued to evolve significantly since its origin less than a decade ago, with an array of variations adopted throughout the world.

The power of an accelerator model is that it brings a group of companies together for a short period of time in one place. As a result, mentors and investors have an easy focal point and can aggressively engage with the companies. It also rallies the community of entrepreneurs, members of the startup community, and service providers around the companies in the accelerator as there is a clear beginning and end to the 90 day process. It's sort of like a MBA program that lasts 3 months and where you end it with funding, solid mentorship and a tangible product.

The accelerator market has grown a lot over the past five years. Most cities have some sort of accelerator program where startups can attend a local program they otherwise would never have been able to go through if the accelerator did not exist. In large cities, there are often multiple accelerator programs. Many participants in an accelerator program are not local to the community where the program occurs, which creates a magnificent opportunity for cross-fertilization of talent and startup experience across the world.

The Global Accelerator Network currently has 70 accelerator programs as members. Members of GAN know that at some level they are competing with each other for companies, talent, and investors. But they also realize it's not a zero sum game and that the evolution of the startup community worldwide along with better understanding of how to start and scale companies, benefits everyone involved. The philosophy of collaboration across the global startup ecosystem is powerful and a deep part of our value system. We are honored to have a network of accelerators with this mentality and continue to work hard to incorporate it into everything we do.

Over the past few years, specialization within accelerators, especially when tied to the strengths of the local startup community, is becoming a key part of accelerator programs. For example, Surge, which is based in Houston, Texas, has a specific focus on energy-related companies. Houston is a historic base of a huge amount of energy company entrepreneurship and large company development because of its natural resource base. As a result, there are numerous mentors and investors in Houston who can actively help and support new entrepreneurial efforts.

Large companies have realized that engaging with accelerators are a great way for them to be part of the innovation cycle. Recently, companies like Disney, Kaplan, Sprint, and Barclays have started accelerators in conjunction with Techstars, using the mentor driven model in Los Angeles, New York, Kansas City, and London (their respective headquarters.) Through this model, executives from the large company are mentors for the companies in the accelerator and engage with both the companies and other mentors working with the companies in the program. In addition to gaining insight into what is happening in innovation around their brands and products, this is a great way for the large companies to find new talent and technologies to incorporate into their businesses. It's also a way for these companies to give back to their local startup communities which birthed them in the first place, and establishing more visibility for them both within their community and the broader innovation ecosystem.

As accelerator programs continue to get created, quality is something we pay close attention to. At GAN, we've focused heavily on this, both on making best practices available across GAN, but also by qualifying accelerators before they become part of GAN. To join GAN, an accelerator has to have at least three years of funding, follow the mentorship-driven model, and its founders need to be committed for the long term. Creating and running an accelerator has the same time trajectory as a startup - it takes a long time and a lot of continuous effort to be successful.

While we are less than a decade into the accelerator model, it's clear that it is a powerful way to help create and fund new companies. I look forward to seeing and participating in the innovations in accelerators over the next decade.

*-Pat Riley*

# *ACCELERATE*
# TOP THIRTY

**1** — **Y Combinator**
United States - Silicon Valley

**Y**
(Average funding raised $3.7m, $1b+ in exits)

**2** — **Techstars Boulder**
United States - Boulder

**3** — **Techstars Boston**
United States - Boston

**techstars**
(Average funding raised $2m)

**4** — **AngelPad**
United States - San Francisco

**5** — **Techstars New York**
United States - New York

**6** — **Techstars Chicago** **(Formerly Excelerate)**
United States - Chicago

**7** — **500 Startups**
United States - Silicon Valley

**8**

# LaunchpadLA
United States - Los Angeles

**9**

# DreamIt Ventures
United States - Philidelphia

**10**

# Seedcamp
United Kingdom - London

**SEEDCAMP**
(Average funding raised $850k)

**11**

# Techstars Seattle
United States - Seattle

techstars
(Average funding raised $1.2m)

**12**

# Muckerlab
United States - Santa Monica

**MUCKERLAB**
(Average funding raised $1m)

**13**

# AlphaLab
United States - Pittsburgh

**14**

# Capital Innovators
United States - St. Louis

**15**

# Techstars Cloud
United States - San Antonio

**16**

# Techstars London (Formerly Springboard)
United Kingdom - London

**17**

# Tech Wildcatters
United States - Dallas

**18** ## Surge Accelerator
United States - Houston

**19** ## Brandery
United States - Cincinnati

**BRANDERY**
(Total funding raised
by graduates
$24m)

**20** ## Betaspring
United States - Providence

**21** ## Kicklabs
United States - San Francisco

**22** ## Boom Startup
United States - Provo, Utah

**23** ## RockHealth
United States - San Francisco

**24** ## JumpStart Foundry
United States - Nashville

**25** ## Portland Incubator Experiment
United States - Portland

**26** ## Entrepreneurs Roundtable
United States - New York

**27** ## StartupBootCamp
Netherlands - Amsterdam

INTRODUCTION

20

# HOW TO GET THE
# MOST OUT OF
# *ACCELERATE*

Our goal with this book is not to tell you what to do or what will lead to success, but to provide you with a collection of thoughts from various founders from around the world.

When reading each of the founders' thoughts, ask yourself: How does this apply to me? How does this challenge what I know or thought I knew? Is this startup/situation different or similar to mine? And most importantly, what next steps can I take from this? Excessive highlighting and notetaking is recommended. By the time you finish this book, it shouldn't be resellable. Imagine the opportunity to sit down and talk to any of these entrepreneurs in person; this book tries to give you a taste of that.

At its very best, *Accelerate* can be a treasure chest from which you pick out your favorite and most useful pieces of gold—only you know what you are looking for and what you need. Consider this book for what it is: a chance to dig into and learn about what has worked and what has not for some successful entrepreneurs. Imagine you got a chance to interview hundreds of founders; what would you do with their insight? Now, stop imagining and read on.

VISIT PAGE 166 TO SEE THE LIST OF 230 ACCELERATOR AND DEVELOPMENT PROGRAMS

THE
SOU

# RCE

# THE
# SOURCE

*"There is no such thing as a new idea. It is impossible. We simply take a lot of old ideas and put them into a sort of mental kaleidoscope. We give them a turn and they make new and curious combinations. We keep on turning and making new combinations indefinitely; but they are the same old pieces of colored glass that have been in use through all the ages." - Mark Twain*

The source of a company idea is hard to put your finger on and is often a mixture of personal experiences and environmental forces. I would like to say that my founder's story is typical–that I had a pain point that I wanted to solve for myself, that also was big enough to be a business, but I would probably be wrong. Ideas germinate in so many ways that are unique to the idea and industry, that there is no one way to stumble across a great idea, but many.

In my case, I didn't chase down the problem that I was looking to solve right away. I worked a little and then returned to it when the timing was right.

While at college I was working on a project with an old friend of mine, Daniel Bailey, a sneaker designer and Concept Kicks founder. I was just getting into the world of entrepreneurship at the time. I had some ideas that I was playing with, but I didn't know of any successful entrepreneurs to bounce them off. I thought a good place to start would be the alumni relations department at my university. Since we had 150,000 alumni, I felt there was a good chance that one or two of them would be entrepreneurial and open to speaking. Two months and three meetings with various staff members later, it was clear that the university couldn't connect me with anyone. They either didn't have the right information on their graduates to relevantly connect them with me or strong enough relationships with their graduates where they felt comfortable making an introduction. As I spoke with others I realized that my experience wasn't unique, leaving many students and recent graduates frustrated. This, coupled with the experience I had when applying to work for Estée Lauder, where the hiring manager was coincidently a graduate from my university, were two of the initial drivers that led to the founding of VineUp.

I co-founded VineUp in 2012 with one of the co-authors of this book, Chris Dowdeswell. VineUp helps universities and organizations tackle the problems that I experienced as a student by allowing them to connect their students and alumni for mentoring and career development opportunities, while supporting the institutions' need for up-to-date alumni information. As of today we support universities in the US, Canada, and the UK, as well as 8% of all fraternities and sororities in the US.

# THE SOURCE OF IDEAS

SOMEONE ELSE'S IDEA

YOUR IDEA

SOMEONE ELSE'S IDEA

Tray was born out of frustration with managing our email inboxes. We started out working on a previous product that took the hassle out of group emails. It was through speaking to our users that we began to understand how email affects everyone in their own individual ways.

These conversations were pivotal in driving us towards a new solution; we wanted to find a way we could help people manage their inbox based on how they already work with the services they already use. Tray started out as a few simple tasks that we set up to speed up processes we carried out every day. It was from here we had the idea to turn this into a platform! - *Dom Lewis – Co-founder, Tray.io (Springboard)*

Back in 2010, the engineering team in our previous startup decided to take part in a weekend hackathon in a hot new technology – Node.JS. We were thinking hard about what would be a nice cool tool we'd like to use ourselves in our day jobs that we were missing. We coded up a prototype over forty-eight hours during the hackathon – and the rest is history. We ended up winning the hackathon out of a group of 400 other developers, and the feedback from other developers blew us away. - *Jakub Nesetri – Co-founder & CEO, Apiary (Springboard)*

I used to work at a company called Control Risks, where I advised CEOs of FTSE 100 companies and bank security and compliance departments on how to mitigate risks in emerging markets. I specialized in gathering and analyzing open source intelligence focused on Russia, Eastern Europe, and Central Asia. But this was really tricky to do. The problem is that the information that we need is a complete mess from the format that it's kept in to the different dialects and character sets that are used. So, I decided to create Arachnys to aggregate and translate this data into a searchable format that is simple to navigate and understand. - *David Buxton – Founder, Arachnys (Springboard)*

I literally had to build several 'mailguns' while working on various projects around 2006–09. First, I needed Mailgun while working on pikluk. com, where we tried to make Big Internet more accessible to children. Email for kids was a big part of it. Being naive, I had thought we'd just get it from a hosting company and it was quite shocking to discover that we had to build it ourselves.

Later on, we built another 'mailgun' for a now defunct service called Dunegrass App. It allowed users to interact with our software via email. Blackberries were big back then, and browsers sucked on them, so providing an email interface proved to be hugely popular with the business users. At that time, I already felt that an email API could be a business by itself, and even offered my brother and a few other engineers to start a company around it. The response was: 'why don't you do it yourself?' And why not indeed?

I even had the name for the company sitting on the shelf. Back when I was learning English, I really liked the sound of the words 'nail gun'. It was just so perfectly suited to the purposeful and brutal nature of a tool. All I needed was to change one letter and convince some guy in Brooklyn to sell me the dot com for it. - *Ev Kontsevoy – Co-founder & CEO, MailGun (Y Combinator)*

I had the idea for PastBook when my father was showing me his diaries and photo albums of him in his younger days. Then I thought: will I ever be able to provide the same experience to my (future) son? The answer of course was 'no' because my entire life is digital, spread everywhere on the web on different social networks. That's why I created PastBook: to let people easily save, rediscover, and share their memories, online and offline. - *Stefano Cutello – Co-founder, PastBook (RockStart)*

I had been advertising on AdWords quite intensively the last five years. I was trying different business opportunities while also working as a consultant for small businesses. During that time, I became very well versed in optimizing Quality Score's and created a system that worked almost every time. The problem was that I had no way of tracking my progress, as I applied my system. That's when Chrétien, my co-founder, said he could help me. At first I thought he couldn't. It became a challenge for him. And I was wrong. He did create the tool and it worked great. Then we started to wonder whether others would like to have it. We put it online and the interest was palpable. *- Christian Nkurunziza – Co-founder, Tenscore (FounderFuel)*

Custora Team

My co-founder and I had been working together for a few years on a number of projects, but hadn't yet found anything we were really passionate about. We knew we wanted to build a company together and were trying to decide what it would be.

Corey (my co-founder) was pursuing his MBA and was learning how probability models could be used in marketing applications (e.g., predicting customer lifetime value). I had formerly started an ecommerce company and had some first-hand knowledge of how valuable these kinds of insights could be. Two things got us really excited. First, there was no product on the market to deliver these kinds of insights, and so only companies with immense resources could take advantage of them. We were excited to help level that playing field.

Second, we saw how these insights could be used to deliver more tailored, one-to-one marketing. Since we receive as much batch-and-blast, in-your-face junk mail as anyone, we were excited to help improve that situation. *- Jon Pospischil – Co-founder, Custora (Y Combinator)*

In the late '90s, Roland (co-founder) and I ran a web hosting company called Netherweb. At the time, live chat was essential to our business, but all of the products in that space were designed for big call centers, and none of them met the needs of a small team. Ten years later, we looked around the market and nothing had changed; the same players were creating the same horrible software. We saw a huge opportunity to bring the power of live chat out of call centers and to the hundreds of thousands of businesses that use the Internet to sell their products. *- Ben Congleton – Co-founder & CEO, Olark (Y Combinator)*

The first time I went through Y Combinator was in 2008, a process that gave me a unique perspective on the insides of a lot of different companies. Every one had different ways of measuring what was going on inside their application – most of them hacked together one or two charts and had a list of important numbers on some admin dashboard they created. I later did some consulting for larger companies and they were having the exact same issues.

It dawned on me that this whole process could be abstracted and made much simpler, and that the benefits of such a system would be larger than just the time saved: making analytics and data digging easier would enable a whole new group of people, changing the way people deal with data and make business decisions. Upon realizing that I was incredibly excited about the opportunities and impact that such a tool could have, I started Chartio. *- Dave Fowler – Co-founder & CEO, Chartio (Y Combinator)*

I was dissatisfied in my own career and frustrated with a lack of resources available to help people like me decide what I wanted to do with my life. I wanted advice on how to negotiate a salary and manage a team for the first time. I was curious to learn what a career in fashion, law, or technology startups might be like. And frankly, I had no clue. My co-founders, Alex Cavoulacos and Melissa McCreery, and I realized that there was a tremendous unmet need, and we were crazy enough to think we could solve it.
*- Kathryn Minshew – Co-founder & CEO, The Daily Muse (Y Combinator)*

I've kept a private blog for more than ten years, as I've always found writing for myself to be an incredibly rewarding activity. But this wasn't the public-facing writing that Facebook and other social media encourages today; it was just things I found useful. None of the journal apps I looked at had everything I was looking for – feed import, sync across devices, backup and export, etc. So we set out to re-imagine what a journal could be if it utilized all the capabilities of today's phones and tablets.

Most of us have two overlapping personas – a public one for the world, and a private one that only ourselves and maybe some loved ones know. Thanks to Facebook, Twitter, and others tools, we're great at creating and maintaining our public personas now. But innovation for the private, personal use case hasn't quite gotten the same attention, yet it's still a common need. So that's the need we wanted to address with Everyday.me – to provide you with a safe place to collect everything you cared about, and to curate, organize, and archive for yourself or other loved ones. *- Yu-Kuan Lin – Co-founder, Everyday. me (Y Combinator)*

I was inspired to begin Take the Interview because I recognized a real problem and was able to devise a simple way to solve it. From my own experiences interviewing candidates, I would often know in the first few minutes that a candidate was a 'no' for my organization, but I would still need to interview him or her for thirty minutes to an hour. Take the Interview very elegantly solved that problem by allowing me to get a sense of who a candidate was and ask them my most important questions prior to an in-person interview. This cut down the time spent interviewing and conducting phone screens. Take the Interview continues to solve this problem not only for me, but also for the hundreds of companies that use our service today.

Additionally, I was inspired to start Take the Interview because it requires recruiters, employers, and candidates to consider a new way to leverage technology to streamline the screening process. I didn't want to begin a company in the same space as hundreds of other companies or start a company that was only making lives

Olark Team

marginally better. Take the Interview wouldn't be an interesting company if it didn't dramatically make the lives of candidates, recruiters, and hiring managers better. *- Danielle Weinblatt – CEO, Take the Interview (DreamIt)*

The concept for SwiftPayMD came out of my own experience as a physician in the trenches challenged by a lack of connectivity between hospital systems and those used in provider offices (where physician billing occurs). Due to this problem, physicians are forced to use inefficient, error-prone, paper-based processes that lead to lost revenue and significant delays in payment. Based on our learnings from potential customers, we have discovered there are some interesting opportunities where our proprietary technologies and tools under development can help physicians leverage their practice's historical transactional data to make better decisions that will improve their bottom line, reduce working capital, and obtain faster payments for services rendered. *- David LaBorde – Co-founder, SwiftPayMD (Flashpoint)*

My co-founder, Marcus, also runs another company called Little Bird Electronics. At this company we taught people how to use a microcontroller called an Arduino. We found that the impediments of needing to know electronics, programming, and networking were holding people back from build stuff. The Ninja Block is our answer to that! *- Pete Moore – Co-founder & CEO, Ninja Blocks (StartMate)*

Ovelin Team

Both Mikko (fellow co-founder) and I were guitar dropouts. We realized quickly that all the products and services out there in this space were focusing on the wrong thing. We asked many people around why they succeeded or did not succeed in learning to play an instrument. Almost all 'successful' guitar players said they had a good teacher, while the dropouts said they did not have a good teacher (or no teacher at all). We then investigated what differentiates the good from the bad teachers and found a pretty simple (and maybe even obvious) difference. The good teachers are good at MOTIVATING people to practice. Thus, we wanted to develop a product that would focus heavily on the motivation aspects of guitar learning. And what is more motivating than playing a good game? *- Chris Thür – Co-founder & CEO, Ovelin (Startup Sauna)*

I'm a naturally action-oriented person, which led me to observe that the single biggest pool of untapped natural resource in this world is human good intentions that never translate into action. My background is 27 years working in brand building, marketing, and advertising. I realized there's another equally large, equally powerful and equally untapped pool of resource, which is corporate good intentions. Companies have good intentions too, but just like people, they lack quick, easy, and simple ways to act on them – and importantly, in a corporate context, in ways that actively make sense for and help drive their business. So I decided I wanted to build a platform that would bring together human and corporate good intentions and make it easy to activate them into shared action, against shared objectives, that could produce mutually ownable results and mutual benefit – Action Branding: you are what you do. Our tagline for IfWeRanTheWorld is 'Feel it. Do it. Be it.' And our logo is a heart with a tick, which encapsulates precisely that. *- Cindy Gallop – Founder, IfWeRanTheWorld*

Evry evolved from a number of different ideas, all in the event planning and group coordination space. My co-founder (Patrick Janson) and I are very social people and are always organizing the next group getaway, BBQ, or concert. Email chains, Facebook events, and text messages just weren't cutting it for us. We were frustrated by group texts that we didn't want to be on or sifting through fifty emails to find all the details of an event, and we didn't think that there was any platform out there that allowed users to organize those small to medium sized events that are more private. So that's where we started. We wanted to create a space to plan and invite friends. Ultimately, however, the core value proposition came from a big pain point in our planning process: paying. Everyone jumps on board and loves the idea of a Hampton's share or concert tickets, but when it comes to collecting the cash it can be a hassle. Evry helps solve that problem by first crowdsourcing funds and then transferring them effortlessly to the planner's bank account. - *Vanessa Dawson – Founder, Evry*

With our combined careers in Congress and advocacy, we both deeply understood what was and wasn't working. Rachna and I started POPVOX to solve our own problems. As a staffer, I had been on the receiving end of constituent and policy input to Congress – and technology was making it impossible to distinguish the signal from the noise. I was also hearing amazing stories from constituents and thought that others should hear what Congress hears. When you know more about the real people or businesses that are affected by legislation, it changes the way you look at that policy. - *Marci Harris – Co-founder, POPVOX*

Artsicle came out of my personal desire to collect art and my frustration with the gallery system. It was cold, inhospitable, and often overpriced. I also noticed that most of my friends were not buying original art – and didn't think they could afford to. We realized there was an opportunity

to connect emerging artists with new buyers, growing the market for everyone. - *Alex Tryon – Founder & CEO, Artsicle*

Previous to founding Lover.ly I worked with my sister, Leila Lewis, at her bridal PR firm, Be Inspired PR. A few months in to working with my sister she got engaged and I was the maid of honor. We spent the next eighteen months knee deep in wedding planning and I was able to experience first-hand the highly fragmented nature of the industry: poor search, lack of tools for collaboration, and the frustration around wedding planning in general. Soon after her wedding (three months), I left her firm to begin working on Lover.ly full time with one goal: to make wedding planning easier and more fun. - *Kellee Khalil – Founder & CEO, Lover.ly*

I guess you could say I've been attempting to design things ever since I could hold a pencil. I remember my aunt, who was an architect at the time, giving me scribbles on a piece of scrap paper when I was around 5 or 6 and making me turn those random shapes into 3D objects, which really helped me as I got older to understand 1/2/3 point perspective drawings.

It all converged when I started to play basketball and developed a love for shoes, so for me it was a natural progression to want to design my own. For years that's exactly what I did, I mean ... they sucked ... really badly, in fact ... but eventually I got better and wanted to make a career out of it. - *Daniel Bailey – Co-founder, lup, and Founder, ConceptKicks.com*

I was previously working in a digital agency (with my now co-founder, Andrew) as a senior designer and developer, building websites for many SMEs. At that time we had quite a number of emerging and independent designers coming to us knowing how crucial it was for them to be in the online space, but with very little budgets to afford a website or their own ecommerce store. Andrew and I knew there had to be a better solution for them and quickly realized that if we created a central online marketplace where they could set up a store and list their products for free, then these designers could be selling their products 24/7 to customers all over the world without any up-front costs to put them out of pocket. *- Marianne Sea – Co-founder, Youngrepublic (StartMate)*

The idea for Enterprise Nation came about from starting and selling my first business. That business (Techlocate) was a home-based business which myself and a partner sold within two years of launching. After the exit, I realized there wasn't a website dedicated to people starting and growing a business from home, so that's how Enterprise Nation started life as the home business website, with our first book being *Spare Room Startup – How to Start a Business from Home*. That was 7 years ago and we have since grown to accommodate the needs of over 77,000 members .. not all of whom remain home based! *- Emma Jones – Founder, Enterprise Nation*

Ribbon came about as a solution to some of our own frustrations. The checkout process today is far too long and if there's one thing you don't want friction in, it's that. A bad experience for buyers leads to a lower conversion rate for sellers as well, so neither side is too happy. At Ribbon, we do the transaction wherever the buyer already is, rather than send them elsewhere and risk losing them. That simplicity is very powerful. *- Hany Rashwan – Founder & CEO, Ribbon (AngelPad)*

Before starting my MBA at the MIT Sloan School of Management, I spent a lot of time in England with my wife's family. There, I saw how popular insurance comparison sites were and how good they could be. Sites like MoneySupermarket.com, CompareTheMarket.com and Confused.com were

so popular in England that over half of all direct insurance transactions went through them. When I came back to the US, I was so disappointed and frustrated with the process of getting auto and home insurance that I decided to look into why the markets evolved so differently. What I found led me to believe that now was the time for a company like Leaky to exist. *- Jason Traff – Founder, Leaky (500 Startups)*

I have always had a strong passion for video production and software development since a very young age – as early as elementary school I was programming on our Commodore 64 and started learning TV production shortly after in high school. In college as an undergraduate at Indiana University, I raised $500k to create a fully student-run TV station on campus, a significant achievement which remains today as a leading campus organization giving students real-world production experience. So in many ways it was inevitable for me to end up creating a video software startup!

After graduation I moved to San Francisco to work in advertising as an online media buyer, which was a great experience to learn the ins and outs of the money in advertising. However, I was still tempted to return to the world of video. In 2008 I started a company called VidSF along with my co-founder, Steve Cochrane. The VidSF concept was simple – we wanted to create an online local TV station. We were fed up with how trashy local TV news is these days – almost nobody we know watches it as it seems to be filled with violence, car crashes, and petty politics—and thought we could crowdsource a better version of local TV news.

The initial year of VidSF was spent creating the support structure in order to prove out the concept. We partnered with local newspapers and blogs such as SFAppeal, SFist, and the San Francisco Chronicle, and recruited a network of videographers to pair with blog and newspaper reporters in order to produce video versions of text articles. We soon realized that we had an infrastructure problem – we needed a solution for these videographers to be able to quickly and easily upload this content, automatically apply branding, insert advertisements, distribute to multiple blog and newspaper partner websites and social networks/YouTube, and then evaluate the viewership of these videos across the various devices, services, and websites where views accessed them. Surely there must be a solution to help create an 'online TV station'? But despite our search, we could only find partial solutions, such as online video players, but nothing that would help with the complicated process from start to finish – so we created our own software which soon became VidCaster.

While VidSF was in many ways a success – our network of Bay Area videographers created hundreds of videos for millions of viewers across half a dozen partner publishers – it was still a struggle to make ends meet with local video advertising alone. Further, while working on the VidSF platform, we were receiving multiple inquiries from companies and videographers who were curious how they could use our video distribution software for their own projects. We realized we had created an extremely valuable video tool and decided to pivot in 2010 to sell VidCaster as a standalone offering.

After setting out to create a local TV station, we ended up with a killer business video distribution platform. We're excited to have followed this path, but there's no way we could have guessed this was the direction it would take! - *Kieran Farr – Co-founder & CEO, VidCaster (500 Startups)*

Four years ago I was working at a company where I inherited an AdWords account that needed better ads. The account used essentially the same ad in all ad groups. I didn't have the time to produce and test what was needed so I had ten people in the company write ad copy for me as part of a game to see who was the best. We used Excel to manage it and it turned out that it was a lot of

fun and it scaled. It also turned out that I won all the contests because I had the tactical experience on how to write a better ad. My co-founder also worked there and we spent a few weeks thinking through how a service like this might work. Over the next few months, another co-founder built a simple web-based testing system and we started looking for beta customers to give it a try. - *Rob Lenderman – Co-founder & CIO, and David Greenbaum – Co-founder & CEO, BoostCTR (500 Startups)*

The short version is that a couple of us were locked in high-rise office towers doing work for the big banks as lawyers right after the collapse of Lehman. We'd see billion dollar transactions flying across the globe at work, while watching small businesses around our neighborhoods get the buzzsaw from the credit crunch. It was utterly bizarre how easy it was to move huge sums of money around the world to finance distant companies that might open a new chain on your block, but nearly impossible to finance the coffee shop 50 yards down the block that you went to every day. So we set out to do that – create a way to put money to work to build the neighborhoods we want. - *Jay Lee – Co-founder & CEO, Smallknot (Techstars)*

A few years ago, I was working at another startup in the health benefits industry, which is subject to quite a few regulations. The team was mapping out all of the processes and regulations that we were required to follow. The problem was that Microsoft Visio is really expensive, so we could only afford a license for one person in our small company. So that single license holder would make some changes to the charts, send a PDF version out to everyone else, we'd all scribble our suggested changes on it, email it back, and then he'd have to make sense of and consolidate twelve different versions.

This was a painful process. As a result, I went looking for a better, collaborative solution and was shocked to find that nothing existed. So I built one. *- Karl Sun – Co-founder & CEO, and Ben Dilts – Co-founder & CTO, Lucidchart (500 Startups)*

I started working on distribution at Yahoo! about eight years ago and had the opportunity to touch almost every product at Yahoo! because of the exciting growth the company was experiencing. From there, I went to work at a few startups and heard the same story over and over. User acquisition, distribution, and monetization for any new company or product is hard. Small companies don't always have the right contacts or the financials to compete with the big guys, and so they get cast aside when it comes to doing any type of meaningful distribution deals. There is a lot of competition in the market and getting in front of the end user takes a lot of work. Not that big companies also don't face the problems with user acquisition and monetization, but the hurdle to get a deal done isn't usually as bad. And the other tools out in the market – SEO, SEM, display advertising, etc. – those don't always scale when you are competing for an end user's attention. End users today are very efficient and don't search the way they used to, say 5 or 10 years ago. We have become masters at blocking out ads, which results in a difficult discovery process for new products. There were other services and competitors in the market, but I thought there might be a different approach and so I started Bunndle. *- Maxine Manafy – Co-founder & CEO, Bunndle (500 Startups)*

# bunndle

In 2007 my co-founder and I lived in NYC and had really dated wardrobes. To fix this we would convince fashionable friends to pick out clothes for us, which revamped and improved our wardrobes. Fast forward to 2011, though, and we found ourselves desperately clinging to the same clothes, well past the expiration date. We were overdue for a refresh, but lacked the time and expertise to make it happen. It just takes too much work to look good, and there's only so many favors you can call in to help. If you look offline, it's very common for guys to take their wives or girlfriends shopping with them to tell them what looks good. We wanted to bring this interaction online. So we teamed up with Sarah, who brings deep expertise in fashion and styling, and the three of us started working together on Bombfell to create a clothing service for the majority of guys who just want clothing to be a solved problem. *- Bernie Yoo – Co-founder, Bombfell (500 Startups)*

My co-founders and I are the ringleaders in our social circles. We plan the ski trips, the rec league teams, the weekend nights out. For years we felt the pain of not getting reliable commitment, having to fork large sums of money up front for group purchases, and sometimes not getting paid back. We found the solution to these problems by interviewing over 200 organizers during our customer development phase. We turned the best practices the top organizers used to solve these problems into a product, PayByGroup! *- Camilo Acosta – Founder & CEO, PayByGroup (500 Startups)*

Andrew, my co-founder, and I came up with the idea when we were in college and quickly realized that internships were an essential part of the college experience, but that most students were finding them the old fashioned way, through family, career fairs, or even sites like Craigslist, and that this experience could be dramatically improved. *- Nathan Parcells – Co-founder & CMO, InternMatch (500 Startups)*

I started in campaign politics in the early days of Twitter, building tools to help campaigns drive donations by targeting their social media visitors.

Michael and I realized there was a big idea behind this work – that if you could capture all the context from how people experience the web, and use it to change what visitors saw, you could make websites dramatically more engaging. The big idea behind that was Spinnakr – a little line of code that you drop into your website to make it automatically target each visitor who arrives. - *Adam Bonnifield – Co-founder, Spinnakr (500 Startups)*

It is extremely difficult for independent content creators to become successful. The odds are so low that, of the 5,000 films submitted to Sundance each year – generally with budgets under $10 million – maybe 100 of them get a US theatrical release. And maybe only five of those will make money. That's one-tenth of 1%. So we created MoPix to give those who don't get distribution an option to control their own fate and directly connect with their fans.

Being based in Hollywood, we previously did a lot of work for studios and film distributors so we recognized the opportunity to control direct distribution through digital. - *Ryan Stoner – Founder & CEO, MoPix (500 Startups)*

These days, almost everyone uses social networks. There are social networks specifically designed for our friends and family (Facebook), for our business contacts (LinkedIn), and for those with similar interests (Twitter). But there is no social network specifically designed for the neighborhood, one of the most important communities in each of our lives. There are so many ways our neighbors can help us, but many of us don't know our neighbors, or how to contact them. Nextdoor was created to change that. - *Nirav Tolia – Founder & CEO, Nextdoor*

Prior to Marquee, my co-founders Luke, Alex, and I co-founded another startup where we designed and coded websites for clients. We realized that not everyone needed a website; many people just wanted a way to share nice looking pages with their friends and followers. People were spending a lot of time and money to hire us when they should have been able to create something themselves without needing to code. - *Katrina Brickner – Co-founder, Marquee (Techstars)*

I met my fiancé through a mutual friend, thought about how natural that experience felt, and realized that no one had made a great product out of it yet. And I wanted to build an alternative for my female friends to meeting random people at bars, clubs, or online. - *Nick Soman – Founder & CEO, LikeBright (Techstars)*

Nick Soman

The company was originally founded with the idea of creating a marketing platform to help restaurants reach their consumers.

During our initial market rollout, we had a lot of exposure to the upstream supply chain. We saw that the supply chain, when it comes to sales and marketing, still operates much the same way that it has for the past forty years. Most/all of the promotions are done with people and paper, and a huge amount of marketing dollars are wasted in trying to reach the end client (the restaurant operator). We theorized that a little bit of technology could go a long way, and came up with the idea of a digital marketplace that could enable the distributor's sales force to more effectively do its job. - *Wink Jones – Co-founder & CEO, Mealticket (Techstars)*

We were working on another project (an automatic, contextual, email-driven search engine for internal company data, how's that for a mouthful?). As we built the product and showed it to customers, we realized that before we could help them use email to facilitate better collaboration, we needed to help them use email more effectively. So we switched over to building workflow tools that we wanted to have. *- Alex Moore – Founder & CEO, Baydin (Techstars)*

The idea for Urtak came out of many years of discussion with my co-founder Aaron Gibralter, as well as a very productive summer of intensive reading. Our key realization was that it's impossible for a person to ever know whether they are approaching a problem with the right questions. That's why Urtak is fundamentally about exchanging questions with other people. *- Marc Lizoain – Co-founder, Urtak (Techstars)*

# Urtak

I've been involved with the printing industry since the age of 15 when I was one of the youngest employees ever at Kinko's. After running product and front-end teams in the dot com days, I did a stint as a turnaround CEO of a printing company. Over the course of four years, I tripled it in size and sold it to a large competitor. Next I started a design firm which grew to multiple offices quickly. We were brokering a lot of print work and started looking for a software tool to manage communication and orders with our customers. We could not find anything even remotely adequate and realized we had to 'roll our own'. I was shocked there was no modern solution in an industry this size and, after validating that, decided to focus on this problem full time. You can say it was an 'Aha!' moment, but it definitely came from understanding both the

industry problem and modern technology/models on a very deep level. In other words: insight. *- Vitaly Golomb – Founder & CEO, Keenprint (Funded by 500 Startups)*

My co-founder, Ralph Shao, and I started The Tap Lab right out of college (Boston University). We started the company because we saw a huge gap in the market. Back then, there were all of these gamified social utilities and local deal finders like Foursquare and ShopKick on the market. But there were no real games out there that thrived in reality. We saw the smartphone as a new platform with a ton of amazing capabilities that game developers seemed to be overlooking. As avid gamers, we knew what we had to do. *- Dave Bisceglia – Co-founder & CEO, The Tap Lab*

Matthew Waldman

I was doing corporate identity and interaction design before the dot com bubble was a bubble. There were no information architects at that time. I therefore set out to retrain myself to focus on intuitive design processes over exercises in aesthetics. To me, interaction design is not limited to the screen, and I re-examined everything my hands and eyes interacted with. I began a re-examination of the complexities of base twelve math versus base ten math for time telling when I came across a large old wall clock in a hotel in London and decided it would be a great paradigm to examine and make truly intuitive. That exercise became the line of timepieces NOOKA is best known for. The idea for the brand was to create an entity that was geopolitically agnostic – a borderless global brand that communicates the optimism of futurism [and techno-progressivism] to the widest possible audience. - *Matthew Waldman – Founder, NOOKA*

Through the years I have spent a large portion of my time engaging with a lot of small businesses, and I have definitely developed a passion for helping small business. It's really easy and relatively cheap to start a business nowadays, which is brilliant, but one thing that has not been democratized and is still very much archaic is the law. Creating strong legally binding partnership agreements, stock option plans, etc., is not cheap. Most startups don't have the $5k to spend on a retainer or a spare $500 an hour to drop on attorney fees. So I decided to start DocRun, an artificial intelligence that replicates about 90% of what a lawyer does but at a fraction of the cost. - *Jennifer Reuting, – Founder & CEO, DocRun*

Together with Ciprian Mardare, my co-founder, we spent nine months working for a job search engine and we found that job boards are not reliable due to the high number of applicants and questionable quality. Recruiting agencies are extremely expensive and they don't always perform as expected.

The best candidates are hired through referrals from employees, so we decided to move this offline behaviour to online by creating a platform where employees can easily refer their friends for positions. Nexi is short from nectere, which means connection in Latin. - *Cristian Andreica – Co-founder, Nexi (RockStart)*

ParkMe began in 2009 as a backlash to the daily frustration of trying to find parking in Los Angeles. We live in one of the biggest car-consuming cultures in the world, where traffic and parking congestion is a part of daily living. What we found when we first started is that the city lacked a sufficient technological solution helping people understand where the spots are in real-time. LA was not alone, most of the major cities in the US

were lacking a credible system for people to use. - *Sam Friedman – CEO, & Alex Israel – COO, ParkMe*

I had experience in the music industry and knew that the weekly CD sales data that labels, managers, and agents were relying on to make decisions was outdated. The way my peers and I were consuming and purchasing music enabled activity to be tracked on a much more specific basis. In 2009, the year we launched, Myspace was the big site and immediately started working with dozens of band managers to make sure the data we were collecting, and the way we were displaying it, was valuable and useful in their day-to-day lives. - *Alex White – Co-founder & CEO, NextBigSound (Techstars)*

Alex White

My co-founders have been struggling with storing and analyzing time series data for over a decade, in everything from automotive, to defense, to renewable energy. While trying to build scalable applications to make sense of the time series measurement data they collected from NASCAR engines, fighter jets, and geothermal energy systems, they broke every open source and commercial database solution available. So we decided to build our own time series database and deliver it as a cloud service for other developers. - *Justin DeLay – Co-founder, TempoDB (Techstars)*

TempoDB Team

We had actually been working together as a company for three years on a different project (a SaaS video platform for sports), but always kept our minds open to new ideas and changing markets. Actually, when we started the first company, we even said, 'We're probably going to change what we're working on.' So with that, we saw the explosion of video, the impact of social and the rise of the tablet, and realized there was a need for a personalized channel to sort through all the noise.

The actual ideation process started with a small team, whiteboards, sticky notes, and caffeine. We essentially started really, really broad and then worked our way down to a simple idea that we could execute quickly (we built our MVP in five days). - *Reece Pacheco – Co-founder & CEO, Shelby.tv (Techstars)*

I think brainstorming is a bad way to build a business. The world doesn't need more fart apps. We need solutions to real-world problems.

Precog comes directly from pains I experienced working as VP of engineering of SocialMedia.com. We had a massive amount of data, and most of it didn't have a rigid structure or fit into legacy systems, so we had to write a lot of code and spend substantial engineering resources to get the analytics we needed to power our advertising platform. Even at that time, I thought, 'There has to be a better way.' I'm building that better way with Precog. - *John De Goes – Founder & CEO,*

## Precog (Techstars)

Before Thinkfuse was called Thinkfuse, it was called ThisWeekLastWeek. I had wanted to build this idea ever since interning at Google in 2007. They have a a great internal system at Google for sharing status among teams called Snippets. I thought I could improve on the core concept of sharing status in a more general sense and purchased the ThisWeekLastWeek domain in late 2007.

Google is also, coincidentally, where I met Brandon, my co-founder. We had decided we wanted to do a startup together and began work on an entirely different idea that had nothing to do with Thinkfuse. That startup was called Classlet and was an app to assist educators with course management at schools. We started work on Classlet during our senior year of college and spent the next two years developing it. It was a side project while we finished up school and then got full-time jobs.

We wanted Classlet to become more than a side project and started finding our way in front of investors. We were told by a number of investors that they don't particularly like the education space. Among other reasons, it's tough to monetize and is a very entrenched industry. We eventually applied to Techstars and made it to the in-person interview. Within minutes of sitting down for the interview, we were told that they loved the team and wanted to invest in us, but they didn't like the idea of Classlet. They asked us to come back within two weeks with a better idea and they'd invest. It was good timing because, by that point, Brandon and I were pretty much coming to the same conclusion; it was time to try our luck with a new venture. We had learned a lot about the education space, but it was time to move on.

That night we put together a list of ten ideas that we thought we'd enjoy working on, and then narrowed it down to three that we thought we could easily monetize. ThisWeekLastWeek, from two years earlier, made it to the top three. We

ACCELERATE

started prototyping the three ideas and, after a few days, ThisWeekLastWeek took the lead and we ran with it. Andy, the Managing Director of Techstars in Seattle, immediately loved the idea. He has to deal with receiving and writing status reports every week, so he immediately understood the pain point that we were solving. - *Steve Krenzel – Co-founder, Thinkfuse (Techstars)*

The idea came from my own experience building mobile apps. I was part of a very small startup called Etacts that got acquired by Salesforce in late 2010. I joined Salesforce but I was really itching to start something of my own. So I spent a lot of my free time in early 2011 learning the mobile landscape and building experimental apps. I eventually left Salesforce because I had been accepted into Y Combinator. While I was building these apps, I realized that I wasn't very passionate about building apps, but that there was a huge opportunity in making it much easier for others to do so. - *Ilya Sukhar – Co-founder & CEO, Parse (Y-Combinator)*

ADVIC

APPLYI

AN ACCE

E FOR
NG TO
LERATOR

# ADVICE ON APPLYING TO AN ACCELERATOR

*For the introduction to this section, we asked Alex Iskold, the Managing Director of Techstars New York, to provide his insights into how to effectively apply to an accelerator program. Previously Alex was Founder and CEO of GetGlue (acquired by i.tv), Founder and CEO of Information Laboratory (acquired by IBM), and Chief Architect at DataSynapse (acquired by TIBCO). Alex created GetGlue, the leading social TV network, backed by Union Square Ventures, RRE Ventures, TimeWarner Investments, and Rho Ventures. GetGlue was named breakout startup of 2011 by Mashable and Top 10 Video Innovator by FastCompany. In 2012 Hollywood Reporter named Alex among the top 50 digital power players. Here's what Alex had to say about the application process:*

While each accelerator has its own characteristics, the application and evaluation process has many similarities across programs.

In the case of Techstars New York, we typically get about 1,000 different applications for each program. These applications start coming in about three months prior to the beginning of the program. While many of these companies are ones we've never heard from before, others are ones we have proactively reached out to and asked to apply.

We consider every application but try to narrow down the universe of companies we consider for each program to 100 companies. We then take those 100 companies and put them through several rounds of interviews, face-to-face when possible, and online when not. These interviews typically run for 15 minutes and involve a short presentation of the company and an intense Q&A from a screening committee consisting of Techstars managing directors and key mentors to the specific program.

We use this to narrow down our selection set to 20 finalists for around 10 slots in the program. The managing director of the program (in the case of Techstars NY, that's me) then spends more time with these 20 finalists, extending offers as appropriate. Techstars doesn't have a hard cap on number of companies in each program, but we aim to have 10 companies per program.

We look for a number of things throughout the selection process. First, if the application is sloppy or half-baked, you're out, as we view this as our first real interaction with you. If you don't take the application seriously, we are skeptical that you are going to take your business seriously.

Great applications have a video demo of the product and often go far beyond the simple questions we ask on the application form. The vision, and the founders' articulation of their vision, is more important than the one-liner about what the company does. But start with a clear one-liner, as it allows me to quickly understand what your company does. Then, show me your progress. Show me user adoption. Show me how people actually use your product. Or, if your product isn't in the market yet, tell me how you think people are going to use your product.

We love to see progress from the point at which you apply through the entire evaluation process. If your company has been around for five years and you still haven't built and launched a product, that's not good. If your company was founded three months ago and you already have five customers, that's awesome.

The background of the team matters a lot. While where you've gone to school and where you've worked is helpful context, we really want to know what you've done in the past. Be specific about your work and accomplishments, not just your pedigree. At Techstars, we often say the most important part of the application is people, people, people, and then the idea.

When it comes to applying for an accelerator, you should know why you are applying. You should have clarity about what you want to get out of the accelerator program. One of your goals is probably funding, but that's more of an outcome of participating in an accelerator. What are your milestones for your product and business progress? If you don't have product-market fit, your primary goal should be finding this during the program.. If you have a business with product-market fit already, your goal might be to increase your network and customer exposure. Or, if you feel you are making solid progress here, a different goal would be to iterate on the product and gain huge user adoption.

The importance of accelerator fit, specifically figuring out which accelerator is best for you, can't be overstated. There are hundreds of accelerators out there, so the accelerators you apply to should address the specific goals that you are hoping to achieve. Too many people look to accelerators just for funding or exposure, and end up with a disconnect between what the accelerator can provide and what the founders need and value. Understanding the differences between the programs, their benefits, and the philosophy of the program, is far more important to your company than simply getting funding.

*-Alex Iskold*

Oh boy. Well, one thing is – be persistent. I applied to accelerators eleven times with my previous company, and I was rejected every time. When Alex, Melissa, and I started *The Daily Muse*, we'd given up on the idea. But Rachel Sklar, founder of Change the Ratio and one of our advisors, encouraged me to put our hat in the ring for Y Combinator, and low and behold, they gave us an interview! I was ruthlessly honest in our YC application: we were scrappy as hell, we had fanatically loyal users, and we were going to build this into a big f***ing business regardless of whether they funded us or not. Luckily (for us both), they did. *- Kathryn Minshew – Co-founder & CEO, The Daily Muse (Y Combinator)*

I think the thing that helped us most was the strength of the connection between me and Corey (Co-founder). We have worked together for years, built things together, and have a strong friendship. Paul Graham has explained why this is important saying 'If you have a strong friendship with your co-founder, you're less likely to quit when things inevitably seem impossible. Friendship will force you to stick on longer than a rational person would, and this is exactly what you need when building a startup.' Additionally, one thing I think helped us was how we went about validating the business before writing a line of code, we had people asking us what we were building. One of the biggest reasons startups fail is because they never build something people want — we weren't at risk of going down that path. *- Jon Pospischil – Co-founder, Custora (Y Combinator)*

I'd say definitely talk to alumni who've gone through the program and get their honest feedback – the good, the bad, the whole deal. No program is perfect for everyone, so you really need to figure out whether program X is right for you. Also, alums will have more insights on 1) whether accelerator X really helped them, and 2) what accelerator X is really looking for. Most people are happy to talk about their accelerator experiences, so you just need to reach out and find them.

   Aside from that, general advice would be: 1) have a working product, or prototype – nothing is a stronger pitch than a live demo that make

people go 'Wow'; 2) build a great team – have co-founders that are strongly skilled in certain areas and complement each other; and 3) show traction – traction is the trump card. If you have 10 million users or X million revenue, everyone will want to talk to you. *- Yu-Kuan Lin – Co-founder, Everyday.me (Y Combinator)*

Pete: Build as much as you can beforehand. Understand as much as you can about your customers. Show that you've talked or sold to as many people as you possibly can before walking into a room and applying. Progress like that is just helpful for building a product in general and also really shows that you're serious about what you're doing.

Dan: One of the Y Combinator sayings that captures what Pete said really well is, 'build something people want.' There are many parts to this. First, build something – don't walk in with just an idea, but actually have built something to prove to the partners of Y Combinator that you actually can build something. Also, build something people want. Make sure what you're building isn't just yet another cool way to share photos on your phone, rather something a user will want or a company will pay for. If you can prove those two things, then you should have no trouble getting into an accelerator. *- Pete Koomen and Dan Siroker – Co-founders, Optimizely (Y Combinator)*

You should launch and get your first paying customer before applying. Some businesses get to that point rather quickly and others take more time. Take that risk out of the equation, and get to that milestone before applying. That way when you're in the program, you've got the basics down, and you can focus on growth. Get paying customers! *- Matt Colyer – Co-founder, Easel (Y Combinator)*

I'd recommend for anyone starting out to really look at why they want to be an entrepreneur, what it means to them, what they'd like to accomplish, and what it would mean if they failed (the likely outcome). The accelerator program is just a kick start to your company, which is just a kick start to your career as an entrepreneur. The accelerator program will last just a few months, but your company will hopefully last many years, and your career as an entrepreneur may last a lifetime.

Having that long-term outlook and a good foundation for your motivations will be essential in making it through the roller coaster you're about to ride. If you take that serious and long-term look at your objectives as an entrepreneur and decide that it is the path to go down, start working on your vision. If you have passion, talent, and a great work ethic, it should only be a matter of time (and applications) before you're accepted into an accelerator program.

Also, when you feel you're ready, reach out to some people who've gone through the program and ask them if they'd spare a few minutes to review your application. You'll be surprised how many people will be willing to help and give you honest feedback, and that'll take you a long way. *- Dave Fowler – Co-founder & CEO, Chartio (2xY Combinator)*

Be a cockroach. Basically have the attitude that you can't be killed, regardless of this accelerator or that accelerator, and that you're going to get there and build a successful company. When accelerators smell that, they should want you. At least I think that was true for us and that's still true for us today, 2.5 years later. *- Rickey Yean – Co-founder, Crowdbooster (Y Combinator)*

Accelerator programs have grown quite a bit over the last three years, but I don't think the standards have changed, at least for YC. When my co-founder and I were going through the process, we only had a few days until the application deadline, so all we had was some crazy idea written down in a text file. If you have more time than that, the advice I usually give is to build a) your founding team, and b) the initial version of your product. I think there's a heavy emphasis on team because smart people that can work well together can build anything they want. After that is solved, and if you can build your product and test it on some users, you'll already have a head start on half the applicants. It also doesn't hurt to have alumni from the accelerator program use your product. A good referral can go a long way. *- James Fong – Co-founder, Listia (Y Combinator)*

Convince them that your company is going to be a success. An accelerator is an investor. Unlike most investors, their main contribution is time and support, not money, but they're still investors. How do you do that? The best way is to clearly articulate why you think you're going to be successful. After all, you and your co-founders are the company's biggest investors: you'll be spending years and tens of thousands of hours building it. Why do you think that's a good idea? On a practical level, take the time to carefully write your application. Make sure it's clear, succinct, and doesn't leave anything out. Your writing needs to compel the partners to give you an interview over thousands of other applicants. *- Ben Lerner – CEO, DataNitro (Y Combinator)*

Listen, learn, and leave your ego at the door. No matter how many TechCrunch articles you've read, you probably don't know what you're doing. There will be people who are part of the accelerator who have done this before and, just when you think you won't make the same mistakes as them, you probably will. Listen to their advice, be a sponge, and use them as much as possible. Remember, don't ask, don't get. *- Dean Fankhauser – CEO, Nuji Ltd (Seedcamp)*

Be yourself! Talk about why you started the company, and try to relate it to your own experience, so they know where you are coming from. If you have any traction such as user growth, engagement level and so on – show them! Be prepared to answer how big is the market size and ideas on how you are going to tackle it. Last but not least, always look for a co-founder or two to join you because they will be expecting it. *- Jack Tai – Co-founder, Notesolution (FounderFuel)*

There has to be something worth accelerating first and foremost. Any entrepreneur looking to get into an accelerator program should build their business until they can show that it has potential, that the market is there and that the market needs the product. It has to be something worth accelerating.

Every business is not made to be accelerated either, so it's good to take a good look at your business and decide where you want it to be in five years, and how you want to get where you want to be. If you don't need acceleration, then why bother? Slow is sometimes better. *- Christian Nkurunziza – Co-founder, Tenscores (FounderFuel)*

Have focus and know what you want to do the accelerator for, and what you want to get out of it. Going in with this in mind will be hugely helpful. Speak to those running the accelerator and understand the process in detail, and who will be assessing the companies to select who will take part. And try and speak to companies who have been through the process. Be serious about the business, and recognize that there will be a huge amount of hurdles. Having a strong team to deal

with those is essential. *- Jude Ower – Founder, PlayMob (Springboard)*

Figure out a way to do an informal Q&A session with the managing partners or decision makers prior to the application process. I had a great call with Mark Wachen, who is the managing partner of DreamIt New York, before I applied for the program. When my application came in, he recognized my name and my company and I was able to demonstrate traction and development from the time we spoke to the time of application. *- Danielle Weinblatt – CEO, Take the Interview (DreamIt)*

#1: Have some sort of prototype or MVP ready. Show that you're not only able to think of good stuff but that there is a huge need out there and you are able to satisfy it. Be creative – a prototype or MVP can have many different forms, it doesn't necessarily have to be a working demo or piece of hardware.

#2: Be honest. If you're already an expert in the space you're trying to get into, use the knowledge and brag with it. If not, than say openly that there are still some questions that need answers. Either way, keep the level of bullshit as low as possible.
#3: Have a great and balanced team. Easier said than done as there is no golden recipe for building one. *- Oliver Lukesch – Co-founder & CEO, Weavly (SUBC)*

Vision and a kick ass team! I can't overstate how important having a great team is. In a tech accelerator like FounderFuel, it was mandatory to have a technical founder; but also demonstrate you guys have a personality.

One area that is underrated is the product. YOU NEED A COMPLETED PRODUCT. If you can't, get as close to a product that you can demo as possible, even if it doesn't work. *- Jeremy Easterbrook – Co-founder & CEO, Prestopolis (FounderFuel)*

Talk to every entrepreneur that's been through an accelerator that you can get your hands on. And practice your pitch. Just do it. *- Boštjan Špetič – CEO, Zemanta (Seedcamp)*

## 'Making a kick ass fax machine is not going to excite anyone.'

An accelerator program is definitely something every entrepreneur should experience at least once. But, keep in mind that not all accelerator programs are created equal. Make sure the goals of your company align with the goals of the accelerator program you're applying to. Are you looking for funding or to get your metrics right? Different programs focus on different things. *- Mikael Cho – Co-founder & CEO, ooomf (FounderFuel)*

An accelerator program can be a huge launch pad for many, but it might be a waste of time for a few. It's ideal for young entrepreneurs and their early-stage startups. You should analyze the need gap and chalk out your deficiency-strength matrix. This helps you decide and grasp exactly what you need from the accelerator's mentorship and workshops.
    Accelerators are like master keys, but it doesn't really make sense unless you're sure which locks you want to open.
    As far as applying or preparing to get into an accelerator program (speaking of India in particular), you should be clear about what dent you want to make in your market and what FUTURE you seek. It's OK to be 'a bit' unclear about how you're going to get there, that's what you get to learn during the program. The right time to apply is when you have an MVP. Also, make sure that you have the perfect team that shares your dream and passion. *- Ankit Gupta – Co-founder, Innovese (iAccelerate)*

I think you should approach an accelerator at a very early stage, sometimes as early as with an idea and a crude alpha prototype of your product. I guess getting selected is mostly a factor of two

major points:

a. Your business idea and its potential
b. The team

Taking a call that early is usually done on the basis of these two points. If the team is great, enthusiastic, driven, and has full belief (basically has the right temperament) then even a weak business idea can be made successful. The accelerator is there to help you shape up your business. So believe in yourself and believe in your idea, that's the only advice I'd give. *- Protik Roychowdhury – Co-founder, croak.it (iAccelerate)*

The early bird gets the worm, so apply early. You don't want to be the thirtieth crowdfunding application that they see. Put all the super-important information at the very beginning of your application, so as to make sure that the reviewers actually see it. Follow up with the accelerator. Being polite can go a long way. Lastly, if you know any of the mentors in the program well enough for them to vouch for you, ask them to write a quick note on your behalf. *- Ethan Austin – Founder & CEO, GiveForward (Excelerate Labs)*

Timing is everything. Flashpoint is geared towards early-stage concepts that have a team in place. This is where the customer discovery process pays the most dividends. Talk to Merrick, Elli, Bess, and others to figure out when the next cohort is and what they're looking for. *- Joe Reger Jr. – Co-founder, Springbot (Flashpoint)*

There are a lot of startup accelerators around now, and a number of them focus on specific types of companies, so do your homework on the accelerators, the value that they provide to their companies, and their expectations for your company. Some accelerators will only work with companies that are nothing more than an idea, while others want to see a group of hackers who have an initial product and some traction. Study the bios of the mentors involved with the accelerators and reach out to those whose skills best compliment your needs. It's like a graduate student looking for the right thesis advisor — the

# 'Don't apply because it's a popular program — apply because it will get you to where you need to be.'

name of the university matters some, but it's more about the best pairing between interests and specialities. **- Howard H. Hamilton, Founder and CEO of Soccermetrics (Flashpoint)**

## 'Not every program is suitable for every company.'

Read the blog posts of companies who were in that program (if they write about their experience), and follow the people running the program (very often they say quite clearly what they are after). If you think it's a good fit, you should join. Do not try to 'fit' your startup into the program. Not every program is suitable for every company. **- Chris Thür – Co-founder & CEO, Ovelin (Startup Sauna)**

Set clear goals for your company as part of the process and evaluate accordingly. For example, if you need to get to a minimum viable product by the end of the program, assess what elements of the program will get you there. If you need to build contacts in a given network, evaluate how the program will build that for you. Don't apply because it's a popular program – apply because it will get you to where you need to be. **-Diane Bisgeier Tate – Manager, Mozilla WebFWD**

Diane Bisgeier Tate

Not all accelerators are created equal, so pick wisely depending on which ones you think fit your product or needs better. For example, Y Combinator is great for more technology-heavy startups and less so for tech-enabled startups (i.e., e-commerce companies); 500 Startups is great for startups that are design-focused and want help with marketing and distribution from its impressive network of mentors, but also have a clear revenue model; Rock Health is great for health-tech startups; while Techstars maintains a smaller class (12–13 startups vs. 80+ at YC or 30 at 500 Startups) in their program so founders get a bit more attention. There's also the Founder Institute (of which I'm a mentor at) that I'd call a pre-accelerator program for people who don't yet want to quit their full-time jobs but want to learn the ropes of entrepreneurship in an evening class format. Either way, my best advice is to (i) get a technical co-founder on your team, (ii) build at least a prototype first and launch it to get some initial feedback/market validation, and (iii) get out and meet other founders or find a handful of mentors that you respect and who can help guide you through the process **- Cheryl Yeoh – Co-founder & CEO, Reclip.It (LaunchBox Digital and 500 Startups)**

## 'Even if you don't get in, the process of pitching, answering tough questions, etc., is going to be good for you.'

Well, if it's only one entrepreneur on the team, I'd say don't bother. There is so much to manage, consider, and interpolate on a daily basis that I can't imagine a scenario where a single member of the team would get through it without getting to the brink of a breakdown. Unless the desired takeaways are purely synthetic, i.e., figures, investment and 'working on your pitch', the real value of an accelerator (if Springboard can stand in here as an example for all of them, which it probably shouldn't) seems to be much more about how a team might develop under scrutiny, pressure, and relentless demands.

If our team didn't triumph the close bonds and plenty of space to have discussions, feedback and huge arguments, I'm not sure that we would have survived the experience. Or else we would probably be called something like ShoppityDoDah – 'making it easy and fast for faster things to happen easier' – or some equally banal catchphrase. I don't mean to make it sound like accelerators promote bottom-line thinking, but rather that fear or pressure can easily take over your vision in an environment that thrives in between polarities: doubt and paranoia on one side, vibrant dreaming on the other.

In brief: keep your team close, and make sure you have extra space available in your mentality, roadmap, and developmental structure to take on board a veritable mountain of new voices saying things you never thought you'd hear about your 'great idea'.

*- Mike Salter – Co-founder & Creative Director, We Are Pop Up (Springboard)*

## 'Attend the Techstars for-a-day program.'

Definitely attend the Techstars for-a-day program, and it always helps if you can build a relationship with, and get recommendations from, a previous Techstars founder. More importantly than that, show that you can ship things, think the fundamentals of the business through, and build traction. *- Todd Silverstein – Co-founder & CEO, Vizify (Techstars)*

HUSTLE – no matter how high the bar raises as the 500 Startups program becomes more competitive, if you have the hustle needed to make your company a success, regardless of what obstacles come your way, you will have a good chance of joining the 500 program. Through hustle you'll

start to knock off the required elements – traction, a great team, and a great product – and you'll find loads of opportunity. In my opinion, there is no greater sign that your company has traction than showing customer growth and tangible revenue. Focus on this and the rest will come. *- Kieran Farr – Co-founder & CEO, VidCaster (500 Startups)*

## 'Have a single killer answer to this one question: why will we succeed?'

We've had the fortuity of being involved with a number of accelerators, both as an accelerated company and being funded by them, and the advice is always the same – the most important thing is to build something that people actually want. If you can do that, you've already solved most of your problems since most startups die from customer indifference above anything else. *- Jason Traff, – Co-founder & CEO, Leaky (500 Startups)*

Make friends with someone already in the program, and keep them updated on the progress of your company. If they are genuinely excited about what you are doing then you'll have a foot in the door. *- Ken Johnson – Co-founder, Manpacks (Seed Funded by 500 Startups)*

Have a product that is easy to understand and can be tested and proven with a small team. If you want to build a new wireless network that requires billions of dollars they are probably not for you, but if you have an idea for a consumer or B2B product that is different then they might be a great partner. *- Rob Lenderman – Co-founder & CIO, and David Greenbaum – Co-founder & CEO, BoostCTR (500 Startups)*

You just have to be yourself. Or at least figure out how to express whatever part of yourself is your strength. Maybe you are annoyingly and relentlessly competitive, or supremely dorky and obsessed about an idea that you can't let go, or you're still on a decades long revenge-kick against the middle school girlfriend who dumped you. If something in you burns, let it be known – you can't hide that stuff and it is as likely to inspire someone as it is to make you look stupid. *- Jay Lee – Co-founder & CEO, Smallknot (Techstars)*

1. Identify the problem you want to solve

2. Spend time researching and validating it

3. Build first version

4. Get your first few customers

5. Measure how you are growing

6. If you are growing then knock on the accelerator's door

7. If you are not growing then work until you are. *- Khuram Hussain – Co-founder & CEO, Fileboard (500 Startups)*

As an entrepreneur looking to get into the program, I think that traction is huge. You should be focused on growing your site regardless of whether or not you are going to apply. If you can prove both that the market is large and that you have the skills to execute and reach early benchmarks then you are in a great place. Also, a key to getting into 500 (or to any accelerator) is to always be building relationships with smart advisors in your space. They can help you stay grounded, help spur new ideas, and help make connections to take your company to the next level. The right advisors are truly invaluable. *- Nathan Parcells, Co-founder & CMO, InternMatch (500 Startups)*

Five simple pieces of advice:

- Be bold and take risks to get on the agenda of the partners of the program

- Have a pitch ready that reflects the values of the program

- Think big about the company you want to build and be ready to articulate that vision with confidence

- Any traction (revenue, growth, etc.) that you have already makes your case far easier

- Enlist the help/advice of other mentors and colleagues connected to the program. *- Adam Bonnifield – Co-founder, Spinnakr (500 Startups)*

Hustle and build. Network with friends who are founders of companies that have gone through the accelerator you are aiming to get in to. Crank out an initial product to validate that you are able to execute your vision. *- Ryan Stoner – Co-founder & CEO, MoPix (500 Startups)*

The right accelerator program will be both the most difficult, and most rewarding, thing you can do for your company. Your team should be prepared to clear their schedule for the duration of the program and to work harder than they ever have in their lives. They should also be prepared for incredible highs and enormous lows; often all within the same day. It's a crazy experience, but we wouldn't take it back for anything. *- Katrina Brickner – Co-founder, Marquee (Techstars)*

Start a relationship with the decision makers early on, and push to get their blunt feedback on how you can improve your business. That's part of what the Techstars program is, so get in the habit before it starts. *- Nick Soman – Founder & CEO, LikeBright (Techstars)*

Start making progress before you get in. The most important thing we did was work really hard during the application period, so that we could show that we were going to be creating good results no matter what. That kind of entrepreneurial spirit makes a big difference. *- Alex Moore – Founder & CEO, Baydin (Techstars)*

Each accelerator is different. Take the time to interview past portfolio companies to learn if the accelerator is right for you and where your startup is at. *- Young Han – Co-founder & CEO, GoVoluntr (500 Startups)*

The accelerator is all about the network, so start early. Get in touch with the founders/managers of the program, speak with alumni (graduates) companies, and get intros to the decision makers involved in the program asap. Basically, make sure that the accelerator program is familiar with you before you go through the application process.

Another piece of advice would be to wait until you have a prototype built. Don't apply with an idea, as competition will definitely bring a prototype or a product. And you will find competition; Rockstart for instance had 354 applications from all around the world. Make something scrappy, put it online, let people use it and improve it. Then prepare a beautiful demo for the accelerator to see. - *Cristian Andreica – Co-founder & CEO, Nexi (Rockstart)*

Cristian Andreica

Do your research and find out who the mentors are, what their backgrounds are and whether they are aligned with what you do. Mentors are a key part of the accelerator experience but some of them will also be involved in the selection process. - *Miquel Ros – Co-founder, GourmetOrigins (OpenFund)*

Hustle, hustle, hustle! Entrepreneurs need to have super thick skin and resilience that would make Pepé Le Pew look like a giver-upper! Read a lot about the accelerator you want to get into, find a way to meet people who are on or have been a part of them (without stalking or being annoying), and then make your company look super awesome when you get a chance to pitch to the people that count. If you don't get in, it's not the end of the world because the most important thing is to make a successful company and you don't need to be part of an accelerator to achieve that. - *Jindou Lee – Founder, Happy Inspector (StartMate and 500 Startups)*

Michele: Focus on the team. Build a great solid team with background covering business, tech, finance, and communication.

Test your idea for as much time as you can before applying. Nowadays there are a lot of pitching events for wannabe startuppers, so I suggest taking some time to travel around nearby events to test your business idea and change it accordingly. Keep your vision strong, but be open to accept criticism and ideas from outside, and work on your most glaring flaws.

Don't apply until you have a distinct market approach, an evident competitive advantage and an outlined roadmap.

Simone: Network as much as you can. Use the events Michele talked about to get to know people. Be bold, don't be afraid to introduce yourself to strangers, be they 'famous' people or other trembling startuppers just like you. Keep those relationships alive, a business card alone is worth nothing. Befriend them on Facebook and drop a line or two every now and then.

Trust me, you get into programs, pitching events and others much more by networking than by mere online applications. - *Simone Pozzobon – Founder & CEO, and Michele Redolfi – founder & CIO, Moku (H-Farm)*

The basic purpose of the interview is for you to prove to the accelerator partners that you will succeed.

Trying to prove something, it is often easier to have a single but amazing and irrefutable argument than a bunch of so-so ones. When walking into that room it helps to have a single killer answer to this one question: why will we succeed? And no matter what they ask just go with it, because that's really the answer they're looking for regardless of the shape and form of the question on the table. Let them know 'we're doing $X/month and growing X% week to week.' Don't hope for them to stumble upon your greatness, show it off yourself. - *Ev Kontsevoy – Co-founder & CEO, MailGun (Y Combinator)*

## 'Accelerators are where you go to accelerate your business, not conceive it.'

Being involved in an accelerator program is an unfair advantage; personally, I don't know how other companies can compete.

First of all, do whatever it takes to get accepted. Wine and dine the admission board, apply to dozens of incubators, whatever it takes. Then to increase your chances, make sure you have a functional product. Accelerators are where you go to accelerate your business, not conceive it. Beyond that, the more traction and users (and dare I say revenue) you have the better. You will have to be a world-class hustler to get in without a product, users, or traction. *- Trevor Koverko – CEO, eProf (CHINA-AXLR8R)*

1. Answer the question: Why you? Any hard problem will have multiple teams attempting to devise a solution. Why are you uniquely suited to solve the problem? What competitive advantage does your team have? Your co-founders are the most important resource you will ever have. Understand as early as possible what each founder brings to the table, and how you are the right team to solve the problem.
2. Engage the accelerator network of mentors, alumni, and leadership. The goal is to form relationships with the folks who can provide feedback on your idea and insight into the application process. References matter, so start early building connections in the network. Don't wait until the last minute.
3. The application is a process, not a one-time event, and progress matters. Seek feedback from alumni on your application early. Submit well ahead of the deadline. Email weekly updates to the accelerator directors. Talk about results from customer development. Share revisions to interface designs. Discuss progress in building your team. The goal is to show forward momentum and that you can accomplish a great deal in a short amount of time. *- Justin DeLay – Co-founder, TempoDB (Techstars)*

1. Market
2. Progress
3. Traction

First, I'd identify a good market that you know well. Making a kick ass fax machine is not going to excite anyone. Second, I'd make sure someone at the accelerator knows you and what you're doing so you can update them if/when you make progress. Finally, you need to make some traction and get customers/users. You need to be able to point to people using your product and loving it. All of these you can do before you raise money. *- Mike Lewis – President & Co-founder, Kapost (Techstars)*

1. Be genuine: mean what you say; make good on your promises; build real relationships.
2. Hustle: there are thousands of other companies competing for a few spots. Hustle like hell.
3. Enjoy the process. Even if you don't get in, the process of pitching, answering tough questions, etc., is going to be good for you. *- Reece Pacheco – Founder & CEO, Shelby.tv (Techstars)*

The good accelerator programs are fiercely competitive. Some companies entering today have made a million in revenue. That kind of boggles my mind. But the three pieces of advice I would give are: (a) don't try to enter with an idea, enter with a product and actual paying customers (it doesn't have to be a billion dollar idea, you can refine it in the accelerator, but it needs to be somewhere in the ballpark); (b) go 10 extra miles with your application, because you need to stand out from all the noise (you're competing with hundreds of other applicants!); and (c) take the time to build and leverage your network before applying, because establishing credibility with the accelerator or friends of the accelerator can only improve your odds of being accepted. *- John De Goes – Founder & CEO, Precog (Techstars)*

Find a co-founder. Most accelerators are skittish about accepting solo founders. Regardless, you should have a co-founder. Doing a startup by yourself is stressful. There will be many days where you want to quit. Co-founders don't simply run a

**MOST COMMON PIECES OF ADVICE**

- HAVE A STRONG TEAM
- HAVE AN MVP (MINIMUM VIABLE PRODUCT)
- HAVE CUSTOMERS/ PROVE DEMAND & TRACTION
- GET TO KNOW THE ACCELERATORS' GRADUATES
- GET TO KNOW THE ACCELERATOR'S MANAGEMENT TEAM

company together, they pick each other up when things get rough.

Have a demo, and personalize it (if applicable) for whoever is running your program. It doesn't need to be a functioning app, but anything that demonstrates your vision. It'll go a lot farther than words on a page.

Statistically, you won't get accepted. A very small percentage of applicants get accepted to accelerators like Y Combinator and Techstars. If you get rejected, don't let that stop you. Keep working on the startup. The worst thing that happens is you simply apply again in a few months.

Quit your job and start your company before you send in your application. Accelerator programs fund nascent startup founders, not wantrepreneurs. Startup founders are inherently risk-seeking and self-motivated. If you're sticking with your cushy day job and waiting for somebody else to give you permission to start a company, then you're not a startup founder, you're a dreamer. Make the accelerator's managing director think, 'This train is leaving the station with or without me, I better not miss it.' *- Steve Krenzel and Brandon Bloom – Co-founders, Thinkfuse (Techstars)*

1. Don't spray and pray. Choose the one or two programs that you think will deliver you the greatest impact and focus on them. Your passion for their program will come across in your application and interview.

2. Believe in what you do, but be open to change. They want to believe that you're determined but also pliable.

3. Team. It's probably one of the biggest deciding factors. You don't need to have a strong pedigree, just show how you kick ass, especially together. *- Dana Severson – Co-founder & CEO, Chasm.io (AngelPad)*

Our main advice is to keep most of your focus on building your company. Applying to accelerators can take a lot of time. That process distracts from the important work of building your business and ultimately makes you less attractive to the programs. If you build a solid company foundation, accelerators will take notice, and you'll find it's a lot easier to get in. That said, one of the key drivers of entrepreneurial success is the team. It's hard for the leaders of accelerators to evaluate teams they don't know. Being part of the entrepreneurial community wherever you live helps expose you to people who can vouch for you and lowers the risk for the people who run the program. *- Miro Kazakoff - Co-founder & CEO, and Tom Rose – Co-founder & CPO, Testive (Techstars)*

MARKE
US
ACQUI

TING &

ER

SITION

# MARKETING &
# USER ACQUISITION

I jumped on my computer this morning to figure out when I'd have time to write this introduction to the Marketing and User Acquisition section you're reading now. I typed in my password and I was immediately faced with my desktop from the night before—Chrome with twelve opened tabs of news, emails, project deliverables, new services I was considering, a recipe I was planning to cook for dinner, and a pair of shoes I was considering buying. I defaulted to starting with email so up came the Gmail tab.

A few emails down was a flyer for Ramit Sethi's BehaviorCon event. I archived it. But, huh, Sethi always says some interesting things on Twitter (this is the mind's associative memory capabilities on full display here!), so up came Twitter with the goal of looking for Sethi's tweets.

Before I got there, I saw a tweet with a link to a "Letter to Craig Newmark." It was a petition by Krrb.com's CEO, George Eid, attempting to convince Newmark to allow his product, Krrb, to integrate with Craigslist. I decided that I didn't want to sign the petition, but Krrb seemed like a pretty useful product. Off to the Krrb site! After watching their one minute introduction on how to use it, I realized that it was really quite simple. I was just about to sign up for their free trial, but my iPhone pinged reminding me I had a meeting in 15 minutes that I needed to prepare for.

The point of this brief chronicle is to exemplify the difficulty of getting an average Internet user's attention; there are so many things today that distract, hook, and catch attention. As Ryan Holiday mentions in this section, "we are living in an attention economy," and boy is it a competitive one. Starting with that in mind should prime you enough to absorb, relate to, and subsequently apply the marketing and user acquisition advice you're about to read. This chapter contains anecdotes and advice from various founders about their experience and lessons in branding, acquiring early usership, leveraging social networking platforms, how to get press, leveraging their product itself to entice bloggers, importance of UX, avoiding time sinks, referrals, surveys, cold approaches, inbound marketing, press events, and maybe five to ten other extraordinary vignettes of marketing wisdom. Enjoy.

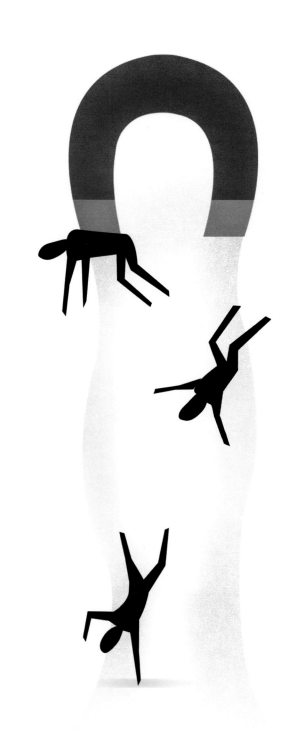

# 'Finding a macro trend and demonstrating how something your company does ties into that trend, is really helpful to reporters.'

We've been really lucky in a lot of ways. First, we create our own buzz wherever possible. I write a column on INC, and *The Daily Muse* content regularly appears on Forbes, Yahoo!, and Business Insider. I worked on each of those partnerships for months, and often I was turned down at least once (record: four times) before making it happen. I respect people who tell me 'no', but that just means I need to wait a few months, understand why what I was asking wasn't worth saying yes to (or who might be the right person to say yes), and trying again. I'm very determined.

In terms of getting covered by others, we work hard to contribute to the tech community in positive ways, beyond just seeking exposure. I founded and ran a previous company with my co-founders before *The Daily Muse*, and though we never got an ounce of exposure, it was a great learning experience for (among other things) how to pitch and present your company. Finding a macro trend and demonstrating how something your company does ties into that trend is really helpful to reporters. Connecting reporters with people who can aid on their current stories, even if it has nothing to do with you or your company. Also really helpful. 'Be helpful.' **- Kathryn Minshew – Co-founder & CEO, The Daily Muse (Y Combinator)**

## 'Everything is marketing.'

1. Be who you are. I can't tell you the number of times in my career someone has said to me, 'We want to be a brand' – and my response is, 'You already are'. Everything that brands you

Kathryn Minshew

flows out of the fundamental truths of who you are and the nature of the business you want to build. So start there, understand who you are as a startup – the sum of the founders' characters, your own idiosyncrasies, your shared sense of humor and your shared vision – and be utterly authentic in understanding and leveraging that as the foundation of your brand.

2. Communication through demonstration. Don't tell people about your brand and your startup. Do things that demonstrate how unique, innovative, and distinctive your brand and your startup is. Everything is marketing. The way you pitch investors, the way you hire, the way you design your business in terms of the way you choose to do business – everything communicates. Design your business cards so they start a dialogue the minute you hand them out because of the way they look and what they say – 'Ooohhh, what's this all about then?' That's what gets you talked about. (This is, obviously, what I mean by Action Branding. My own startups are built around my own beliefs and values, and I live my own philosophies.)

3. Don't give a damn what anybody else thinks. My favorite quote of all time is Alan Kay: 'In order to predict the future, you have to invent it.' I'm all about deciding what you want the future to be and then making it happen – which is what every startup is about. But it's really, really hard to invent the future if you care too much what anybody else is thinking – your friends, your family, the startup community, the investor community, the business world, the trade press. You need not care what anybody else thinks. That way, you can be sure you are always doing what is really right for your future-forward concept – and you'd be surprised how much you stand out from the crowd when you really don't care what anyone else thinks, and how much people will talk about you accordingly.- **Cindy Gallop – Founder, IfWeRanTheWorld**

Cindy Gallop

The three-step core practice of inbound marketing: 1. 'Get found' (top of the funnel); 2. Convert (middle of the funnel); and 3. Analyze (analytics). Take a moment right now to check exactly how well you're doing on these by putting your URL into marketing.grader.com. Create a free account, and there you can track your progress and get new tactical tips every time you log in. Meanwhile, I'll explain each step:

1. Get Found. Nobody's going to find you in the first place if you're not making yourself useful by generating and sharing content that people need. Write about the types of problems your company solves. Write about the stuff someone you're trying to reach needs to know to get their job done. Create great content that indexes well in Google because it actually provides a service and helps people solve their problems.

2. Convert. You need to do something that helps the people coming to your site and reading your content get more closely involved with the company. This could be earning their contact information with a really great piece of content. It could be nurturing them as a lead by sending them additional relevant, useful, targeted content after they first 'convert' on a form or offer or social channel. You need to get them from 'I have this problem' to 'wow, this company could solve my problem' and you need the patience to make that process more about them than it is about you.

3. Analyze. All of the above are going to take forever if you're not measuring the right things, or if, heaven forbid, you are not measuring at all. At each step, make sure you're using software that tells you how the tactic performs and shows you how those metrics connect to all of your other marketing. That's not a pitch, by the way, there are many free and inexpensive pieces of software you can thread together to do this on your own. HubSpot just puts 20+ of these tools all in one end-to-end, fully integrated dashboard to help you stay on top of things more efficiently. **- Laura Fitton – Founder, oneforty, and author of Twitter for Dummies. Currently Inbound Marketing Evangelist at HubSpot**

*'Don't talk about features; talk about solving problems.'*

'Focus' is a really good word. I love it. I have two pieces of advice regarding focus that will instantly make your marketing more impactful. First, focus on what your users want and what benefits your product is providing. Don't talk about features; talk about solving problems. Don't talk about yourself (too much); talk about others (much more). Find twenty-five things you can use to educate, entertain, or enlighten your current and potential users. Then create epic content about those twenty-five things. I learned this framework from Corbett Barr (thinktraffic.com) and it works like magic.

Next, focus on the things that will get you the highest return on investment. For example, if you want more users, think about what are the most effective and efficient actions you take to get them. For web startups, these actions almost always have something to do with either conversion optimization or traffic generation. They rarely have anything to do with the number of Twitter followers you have. Yet, I see founders tweeting until their noses start bleeding and, meanwhile, their sites are in bad shape.

There are several philosophies that I see startups mistakenly embracing. Each one of them ends up either hurting the companies or running them out of business completely, and here they are:

1. The 'build it and they will come' mindset. News flash: nobody cares about your product ... unless you make them care. Nobody will come ... unless you show them the way. There are thousands of companies getting started around the world every year and most of them, quite frankly, suck. As a result, people have learned to discount anything unremarkable, and ignore the constant noise of mediocrity. So if you want to stand out and get noticed, you better start thinking about how you're going to market your company. Because having a great product is awesome, but it's only a part of the recipe.

2. The 'silver bullet' mindset. So many founders these days believe that there is one 'silver bullet' event that will make their company explode. These are the entrepreneurs who can't wait to announce their product at SXSW. They can't wait to get their startup all over TechCrunch. But in reality, no specific event and no single win can make your company successful. Instead, it's a combination of tactics plus a commitment to execute that will get you growing.

Basically, marketing should be kind of like working out. You won't get fit if all you train is your right bicep. You've got to focus on all muscles and keep training for a long, long time. *- Mike Abasov – Founder of MBF*

When it comes to product placement, you need clothing or products that celebrities would want to wear or use. The quality must be there, but most celebrities will be far more likely to support a company that reflects a lifestyle that they believe in or want to be associated with. Gaining access to celebrities is tricky though, especially because there is a specific way it is done in the fashion industry. At the beginning, I would suggest using a PR company like Film Fashion, based in LA. They will work with you on the introductions if you have a product they believe in. *- Jaclyn Sharp – Founder, fashion brand Imposter*

Jaclyn Sharp

> *'It's not that the value proposition has changed, it's that the competition has gotten infinite while people's attention spans have stayed the same.'*

## *'Scarcity helped drive demand; it led to a lot of online word-of-mouth.'*

Initially we had a lot of press; we had really great coverage on our launch; those initial users translated to great word-of-mouth when people started sharing their bios on social media. We also required an invite code on launch. I think the scarcity helped drive demand; it led to a lot of online word-of-mouth. **- *Todd Silverstein – Co-founder & CEO, Vizify (Techstars)***

You can't expect your product to get an audience just because. If you build it, they will NOT come. You have to make them come. And the only way to do that is to be adept at marketing, packaging, and psychology. It's not that the value proposition has changed, it's that the competition has gotten infinite while people's attention spans have stayed the same. To get your share of it you have to win the fight.

You start online and you start with the people who influence other people. Think of it as a force multiplier. You can put all your energy on getting a tiny article in the USA Today that might bring you a few hundred users. Or you can start small with a blog that is read heavily by other blogs and watch as one mention turns into dozens – and thus thousands or hundreds of thousands of users.

Why do you think everyone competes to be on Hacker News or TechCrunch? Those sites are read by a FRACTION of the general population,

so it isn't about users – it's about hype. It's about starting the hype cycle. In the startup world there isn't a huge difference between 'the thing everyone is talking about' and 'the thing everyone is using'. In fact, often times the former ends up cashing out for more than the latter because the latter seems to be boring to investors, even when it's a better and more solid business. **- *Ryan Holiday – best selling author of Trust Me I'm Lying, and director of marketing, American Apparel***

## *'You start online and you start with the people who influence other people.'*

Don't be afraid to try crazy approaches to user acquisition. When we first started out, we gave away credit to large groups of people to get them to try the app. Don't be afraid to make an initial investment in user acquisition, and even more importantly, it pays to implement a long-term strategy that rewards users for recruiting new ones. (We still run a 'give $5, get $5' campaign for new users and their recruiters alike). **- *Seth Priebatsch – Chief Ninja, LevelUp (DreamIt)***

**LevelUp**

We acquired our first users by leveraging our networks, including asking the members of our accelerator program and our advisory board. Once you get your first Beta tester, you can leverage the results from that user to create a case study and acquire others. It helps you develop the self-referencing needed to 'cross the chasm' and helps you better define your target market.

You won't necessarily be able to define your target market immediately, even if you have a successful outcome from a Beta test. Always question the results and assumptions you make about your target customer until you have a series of companies not only using your product, but also paying for it. Your goal in business should be to generate revenue. That's what sustainable businesses do. **- Danielle Weinblatt – CEO, Take the Interview (DreamIt)**

## *'It's about starting the hype cycle.'*

Press can get you a few early adopters. After that, LinkedIn is a great resource for us (B2B says that we sell to digital marketing professionals).

Do not waste time in slower markets that you need to educate rather than sell to: life is too short to spend it convincing people that the Internet is going to be big. **- Gabriel Hubert – CEO, and Stanislas Polu – CTO, Nitrogram (Seedcamp)**

It was important to develop a high-quality group of early users in the beginning, not a large one. From there we were able to define the brand, product and get feedback from heavy users whose opinion really mattered to us. I personally reached out to leading bloggers, asking them to join and give me feedback in return for making them important on the network. This worked surprisingly well.

In the early days it's important to remember that UX is everything to growth. Every important action a user takes on your site should reach people outside of the website's network. For example,

the UX flow that Instagram built into their product was perfect. Every time you take a picture, the last step of the process is to write a comment and share. It was a seamless way to share your photos on other networks. In the beginning of a user's experience, it made more sense to share the picture on Facebook or Twitter than their empty Instagram network. **- Dean Fankhauser – CEO, Nuji (Seedcamp)**

We had a lot of success early on with business development partnerships – partnering with media companies to power ticketing for their sites. We were able to get those deals through because we made it hyper-simple for them to integrate. Whereas most other ticket companies left the burden of the integration on the media company, we did the whole integration for them. **- Jack Groetzinger – Founder, SeatGeek (DreamIt)**

It seems odd to think about it, but Enterprise Nation was launched before Twitter existed, and Facebook was still mainly operating in the US, so social media wasn't our immediate priority. We recruited members through publishing books that encouraged people to visit the site, speaking at events across the UK, writing for publications, tie-ups with blogs, and sites where our community was hanging out, launching awards to recognise star businesses, a regular newsletter, and creating a friendly place so business owners would visit, feel at home, and then recommend to their friends.

Much of this activity continues today, but we now run our own events (as well as still speaking at others), so this year we will train over 2,000 startups at workshops and publish over fifty eBooks/books/kits that will benefit our members and hopefully attract new ones. Oh, and of course we now use Twitter, Facebook, and LinkedIn too! **- Emma Jones – Founder, Enterprise Nation**

We attended every tech event in both Europe and the US that we could find, and obsessively pitched the product to anyone remotely interested. At the same time, we had frequent releases, that these connections then amplified into pretty efficient PR acquisition. We unfortunately never figured out what virality is. *- Boštjan Špetič – CEO, Zemanta (Seedcamp)*

Boštjan Špetič

As a marketplace we have always seen acquiring users as a stair function, where as a team we are collectively innovating and investing more heavily on one side then the other. When we reach a breakthrough on the side we are working harder on, we then flip over to the other side. In the early days we seeded the platform, as I mentioned above, with employers who signed beta agreements. Our site was just based in Washington state at that point, so we later built relationships with local universities, student groups, and got local press to help grow the student side. As we looked to expand, we focused again on employers and succeeded through a combination of aggregation, SEM and inbound marketing. We then turned to students again and ramped using SEO, business development and larger, more expensive ground campaigns. As anyone will tell you, there is no silver bullet to gaining either student or business traffic, but what is wonderful is that, as a marketplace, the more employers we bring on board the easier it is to attract new students, and the more students we get, many of them report to current and future employers about IM and help us grow that side as well. *- Nathan Parcells – Co-founder & CMO, InternMatch (500 Startups)*

We ran an early contest to find the best guys in Seattle according to women. We had a party hosted by Sir Mix-A-Lot to celebrate the winners, and that drove some fun press and users to LikeBright.
*- Nick Soman – Founder & CEO, LikeBright (Techstars)*

At the very beginning, we did what everyone else did – we sent it to our list of contacts and asked them to spread the word out. That moved really slowly.

We experimented with a few more things until the app was more stable. A few months after launch, we went on AppSumo, which gave us a huge lift in terms of paid conversions. It has always been data-guided decision – A/B testing – inbound marketing – repeat. *- Ai Ching Goh – Co-founder, Piktochart (CHINA-AXLR8R)*

eProf started out as a marketplace. Marketplaces are tough. It takes a lot of time and a lot of money to build a two-sided marketplace. To gain traction early on, we only focused on one side of the marketplace; in our case, the teachers. We catered to the supply side and encouraged them to bring their own students with them. But as I said, overcoming the chicken and egg problem is not easy. In retrospect, we probably should have focused on the demand side (students). They are the paying customers and need to be subsidized in the early days. *- Trevor Koverko – CEO, eProf (CHINA-AXLR8R)*

*'Find the natural place your customers already gather.'*

Go to them, do not expect them to find you. We wanted to group lots of SMB's together who were buying similar products in the same vertical.

However, marketing to SMBs is known to be an expensive and time-consuming endeavor. So we started to look for where they were already naturally grouping themselves together. We found that the best of the best SMB's in America were already members of co-operatives, buying groups and trade associations. We used these groups as our marketing channel to the SMB's, which dramatically reduced our customer acquisition costs and allowed us to launch a new vertical with 500 SMB's ready to go at launch. Most tech companies do not even really know what a modern-day co-operative is. So look where no one else is looking and find the natural place your customers already gather. *- Jonathan Jenkins – Founder & CEO, OrderWithMe (CHINA-AXLR8R)*

## *'All display advertising, search ads, affiliate deals, and retargeting failed miserably.'*

In our industry, no one trusts banks, and for a good reason. It was quickly evident that for a new unknown online player to buy customers with advertising is totally out of the question. All display advertising, search ads, affiliate deals, and retargeting failed miserably. Instead, what worked beautifully was word-of-mouth for building trust and 'wow'-ing your customers every step of the way, so that they want to tell everyone about this awesome new tool/product/app they used. *- Kristo Kaarmann – CEO, TransferWise*

I had connections to about twelve band managers through my time in the music industry, and these were our first users. As we built more product we would be told that 'we had to talk to so and so' and also pressed people to connect us to other 'forward thinking managers'. We built up about 100 users for the pre-launch beta version of our site.

After launching we shifted to an entirely different

strategy. We were written up extensively, providing an initial jolt of signups, but we also relied on a free site where anyone could type in any artist in the world and see data back right away. This proved to be very useful, and in giving away this value, word spread and tens of thousands of people have since signed up to get free weekly email reports on the artist they care to track. *- Alex White – Co-founder & CEO, NextBigSound (Techstars)*

We focused on establishing TempoDB as the time series data standard in the minds of developers who were feeling the same pain that we did. We invested in SEO and content creation to ensure that we were the first solution that developers discovered when searching. Today, we are the #2 result for 'time series database' (behind Wikipedia), and the vast majority of our users come from inbound search. *- Justin DeLay – Co-founder, TempoDB (Techstars)*

For our early customers, it was all outbound; chatting with companies we knew who might have the pain. But for recent ones, it's all been inbound. If your copy is relevant to what you do, then Google is pretty good at helping companies find your website.
*- John De Goes – Founder & CEO, Precog (Techstars)*

Techstars was invaluable with our early user acquisition. From the very first week, all of our peers in our class were using Thinkfuse and giving us feedback. Even better, we leveraged the extensive mentor network that Techstars has to get meetings with managers. Within a week of starting the program, we were meeting with VPs at AT&T, Directors at Starbucks, General Managers at Microsoft, and many other managers at all levels within the company hierarchy. We were getting so many introductions that we actually had to ask them to slow down. *- Steve Krenzel – Co-founder, Thinkfuse (Techstars)*

In starting InternMatch we ended up doing a ton of lean startup best practices, even though we were new to the startup world and had no idea who Eric Reis or what lean startups were. We interviewed hundreds of students on college campuses, but better yet, we developed a massive employer outreach and sales process, where we talked to employers on the phone, setup meetings, and then got them to commit to a Beta contract whereby we would let them use our site (which didn't exist yet) for free in exchange for early feedback. Not only were the meetings incredibly helpful in building our product, pitching to investors, and growing our expertise, but we developed hundreds of early users for when we launched that were all committed to giving us a ton of feedback.

In validating demand we knew that internships were a huge industry (with over 80% of college students completing them) but needed to know just how big the market was for employers and how much the average employer spends hiring interns. Almost none of this data is publicly available, so in the early days we were forced to use back of the envelope calculations to find answers. Finally as we grew and our network got bigger, one day we got connected to someone who had run one for the largest intern job boards that existed before us. This person had spent thousands of dollars to pin down the exact college recruiting market size, which is in the billions and after nearly a year and a half we finally had a more exact number. **- Nathan Parcells, Co-founder & CMO, InternMatch (500 Startups)**

## 'You don't know what you don't know.'

We got some attention from early users after we launched a very early prototype at PyCodeConf, a Python conference we co-sponsored with GitHub, Heroku, and a few other great companies. The product was rough around the edges, but we got great feedback on the features people wanted to see. It was also validation for us that people were interested in what we were building. **- Katrina Brickner – Co-founder, Marquee (500 Startups)**

'You don't know what you don't know' is one of my favorite quotes. In it contains wisdom for life, your career, and most importantly, user experience! In the simplest sense, user insight helps you to know what you don't know – whether it's 'what your most engaged users love or hate' or 'is this even solving their real problem?'

What these founders prove is that user insight serves a very real purpose both before and after your product is done. This is not to say that you should get like an MBA graduate and put out an extensive questionnaire for your ideal customer, nor should you get like Steve Jobs (or what media suggests he's like) and 'forget' about what customers want. From the early stages of trying to figure out what the hell kind of problems your target market really has, to the middle stages of tweaking your value delivery, to the later stages of amplifying your product experience and KEEPING customers, the founders share the methods they've used to acquire user insight as well as some of the things they learned from this insight …

One of the most interesting things that we've learned with Leaky is that, no matter how easy the process is, people would prefer to not have to deal with insurance at all. This led us to develop our 'rate monitoring' service, which will allow registered users to have their driver profile continuously run in the background and to be alerted when we detect a rate drop for them. **- Jason Traff – Founder, Leaky (500 Startups)**

We ran surveys and conducted user interviews. We highlighted some problem statements in our surveys and carefully reviewed which problems were reported the most by the participants. The

benchmark here was if 40% of people agreed to a problem statement then it was worth investigating further. The followed up the themes which emerged by doing interviews. **- Khuram Hussain – Co-founder & CEO, Fileboard (500 Startups)**

We spent over a year in private beta before announcing the service publicly. The entire purpose of this 'stealth' period was to gain as many consumer insights as possible before launching. During that year, we worked closely with over a hundred neighborhoods across the country to create a platform specifically designed to make neighbors feel comfortable sharing information with one another. The most important thing for any company is to be laser-focused on solving problems for its users. As we learned from our launch, when you create a product that people find useful in their everyday lives, the demand and positive response comes organically.

The Pew Research Institute reports that 28% of people don't know any neighbors by name. That is in the real world - in the online world, Pew reports that only 2% of a person's Facebook friends are their neighbors. At the same time, we found data that said that 93% of people believed it is important for neighbors to look out for one another. These three stats validated the demand for a service like Nextdoor. **- Nirav Tolia – Founder & CEO, Nextdoor**

I interviewed 100 women via Mechanical Turk, and found out that the lack of social context is a huge problem in dating. We've been bringing women in weekly ever since to help us shape our product and our vision. Our early research showed a huge opportunity in that 90% of single people don't date online, and most of them do want to date. So we set out to figure out why. **- Nick Soman – Founder & CEO, LikeBright (Techstars)**

We learned that we were on to something when we launched a prototype of our concept at Boston University. The game was called Duality and with it we turned the entire campus into a game of risk. We had 100 students playing the game and the campus transformed into a war zone overnight. The students loved the game and our engagement numbers were very encouraging. With that, we quit our part-time jobs and have been doing this 24/7 ever since.

In the very beginning, we were primarily focused on engagement metrics. How often a player opened the game and how long they played for (session frequency and session length). In our first game, TapCity, our active users played more than twenty-five minutes a day, which is up there with some of the top performing games on the App Store. We tracked the data using Localytics, a top-tier analytics provider based here in Cambridge, MA. **- Dave Bisceglia – Co-founder & CEO, The Tap Lab (Techstars)**

## 'I can't speak strongly enough about the importance of partnerships.'

We were extremely fortunate to have the support of a few strategic partners very early on. Those relationships led to an insane amount of exposure and interest in our platform. We were able to grow our user base by 20,000 in just a few short months. Once that happened, we had momentum on our side.

I can't speak strongly enough about the importance of partnerships. Not only can they serve as a major distribution channel, but sometimes they help establish early social proof and credibility. **- Dana Severson – Co-founder & CEO, Chasm.io (AngelPad)**

'When you create a product that people find useful in their everyday lives, the demand and positive response comes organically.'

# BUSINESS

# NO BUSIN

# PLAN VS

# ESS PLAN

# BUSINESS PLAN
# VS NO BUSINESS
# PLAN

70

A couple of years ago i started a blog called HowToWriteABusinessPlan.com. The blog was designed to be a resource for entrepreneurs, featuring interviews with founders discussing their thoughts on business plans and business plan templates. For early stage technology companies, I got a chorus of no's in regards to the argument as to whether to write a business plan or not. Many that we interviewed for the blog had created very successful businesses and have never written a business plan.

I learned this about business plans the hard way. My first business plan was 68 pages long with 5 pages of financial forecasting and modeling. The supporting evidence? Some really lovely graphics. We were excited about the monster of a document that we had created. However, its contact with investors resulted in a scan of the executive summary, a flip to the team page, then straight to the financials. Months and months of planning and editing were digested in 90 seconds.

When planning for a wedding, a trip, a building, or retirement, with a few glaring exceptions, the plans stay true to their design. However, I have never heard of an early stage business plan that withstands its first contact with customer or investors.

But this isn't to say that you should never write a business plan. Writing one can be a great learning process not just to gain a complete understanding about your business, but also to help formalize the wording for the problem that you are solving, what you're trying to achieve, and how you will go about doing it. As Carol Roth, Author of the New York Times bestselling book *The Entrepreneur Equation*, explains later in this book, "a business plan is a great way to go through the vetting process for an idea and help you work through some building blocks for strategy and execution. It's critical, but it's not a be-all-end-all. You won't replicate the plan exactly and you won't be able to predict the future with 100% certainty."

A business plan is one tool to help entrepreneurs think through key facets of their business and their market. Some alternatives to writing an early stage business plan would be:

1.  Fill in the application form for a top tier accelerator—any of the *Accelerate Top 30* will work for this.
2.  Build a pitch deck (a 10-12 page slide deck that focuses on the core areas of your business).
3.  Create a Business Model Canvas.
4.  Write down your business model in a page or less.
5.  Tell your pessimistic friend about your idea.

## SHOULD YOU WRITE A BUSINESS PLAN WHEN STARTING YOUR COMPANY?

**FOUNDERS OF TECHNICAL COMPANIES SAY:**

75%

NO

YES

25%

**FOUNDERS OF NON-TECHNICAL COMPANIES SAY**

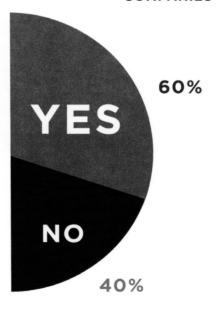

60%

YES

NO

40%

One great way to start is to pitch your idea to five people with some relation to your potential business – future ideal customer, potential investor or someday partner – and ask for candid feedback. What are their questions? Common areas of scepticism? The sooner you can nail down your fundamentals and anticipate outside questions the better. If you have a fuzzy understanding of how you might make money, do research. Exactly how much do individuals or companies spend per year in your specific space? How much of that can you expect to capture? What assumptions would someone have to make about your business to get to $10 million in revenue? 100 million? Call me old-school, but I like businesses that actually make money  Also, getting paid by your customers is really fun! - *Kathryn Minshew – Co-founder & CEO, The Daily Muse (Y Combinator)*

**the**muse

I think the most important thing to understand about a business plan is that it's all about the journey rather than the destination.

A business plan in itself isn't terribly useful. It gets out of date too quickly, and if yours isn't then you aren't experimenting enough. However, the process of creating a business plan can be incredibly useful. It forces you to answer questions you might not be thinking about on a daily basis.

When I've put business plans together in the past, I've found that I end up generating more questions than I answer. However, the great things about those questions is they tell you what you need to do next. - *Matt Colyer – Co-founder, Easel (Y Combinator)*

*'Our goal as entrepreneurs is to get to product-market fit as soon as possible.'*

I don't believe in the notion of 'writing a business plan' in the traditional business school sense. I think the idea of writing a forty-page static business plan is outdated. Real entrepreneurs should think about writing a series of 'assumptions' on the problem, market, and solutions, and set out to run 'experiments' to prove or disprove their hypotheses. This is Eric Ries' concept of how to create a lean startup, and how to think about customer development early on and iterate quickly. A good way to learn these principles would be to participate in a Startup Weekend or the Lean Startup Machine Weekend (of which I'm an advisor and mentor of). You'll find that once you create an MVP or prototype and throw it out there, your assumptions will change, hence your product and business model will too. Your goal as an entrepreneur is to get to product-market fit as soon as possible through a series of iterations until you find a scalable and repeatable business model that the market wants or needs. - *Cheryl Yeoh – Co-founder & CEO, Reclip.It (LaunchBox Digital and 500 Startups)*

Don't start by writing a business plan. Go talk with lots of potential customers, find a problem lots of people have, create an awesome solution and don't be afraid to pivot when needed. Create a business plan once you have a solution that people are paying for that can scale. - *Ivo Minjauw – Co-founder & CEO, SocialExpress (SUBC)*

I have never written a business plan. - *Ajay Meht – Co-founder, FamilyLeaf (Y Combinator)*

I highly recommend reading *The 4 Steps to the Epiphany* by Steven Blank. That book really changed the way I looked at starting a business.

> *'I have a friend who wants to build a business, but spends all his time planning about building a business rather than actually building one.'*

The super-short version of Steven's book as it relates to the first business plan is that you should make a list of all the reasons that you think your business will succeed, and then treat those reasons as assumptions and hypotheses of an experiment. Your job then is to experiment and research to gather all of the information you can to determine whether those hypotheses are correct. If you find that they are not, then you need to shift gears in some way based on your new set of knowledge. It's a continually adjusting experience. **- Dave Fowler – Co-founder & CEO, Chartio (Y Combinator)**

Don't write a business plan unless you really have to. Unless someone has required you to write a business plan, I honestly believe it would be a waste of time to write one. I have a friend who wants to build a business, but spends all his time planning about building a business rather than actually building one. It hasn't taken him very far so far. It's more important to focus on building something first.

If you really need to write a business plan, then I would assume you already have the genesis of a valuable business in place, in which case you won't have much trouble writing a business plan. Find a template online, fill in the details relevant to your company (because you will have already

done all the work), slap it into Apple iWork Pages to make it look beautiful and that's it.

I'm actually going through the process of writing a business plan myself, but I'm only doing it because we're applying for government grants. And since my business is already somewhere, I have no trouble writing it. I know the market, the needs, the marketing strategy, the financial projections, etc. All that is part of the work I did while putting the business in place **- Christian Nkurunziza – Co-founder, Tenscores (FounderFuel)**

I wrote a business plan once, when working on my first company in college, and to be honest I don't think I'd ever do it again. It's more valuable to spend that time getting something out into the world (some form of MVP), getting users, etc. **- Jon Pospischil – Co-founder, Custora (Y Combinator)**

Don't bother with a too detailed business plan. Most likely you don't know enough about your customers and the market – even if you think you do. Make sure that the envelope figure, the total market that you're looking at, is big enough to support the vision of your company. After that, just focus on the product and refine the business plan as you keep moving. **- Jakub Nesetri – Co-founder & CEO, Apiary (Springboard)**

I've been doing startups for a long time – both small bootstrapped businesses and investor-backed companies – and at least in the US, the concept of a business plan has radically changed. If you are doing a venture-backed business, you are better off creating a really strong PowerPoint deck: ten to twelve slides ideally, and/or have an existing site/app/working prototype to show investors. VCs and 'serial angels' are used to seeing pitches in this format now, for better or worse. There are a number of resources online to help create a great pitch deck, and the reality is you really need to spend a LOT of time on it, unless your site or demo speaks for itself. *- Clark Benson – Founder & CEO, Ranker (LaunchPad LA)*

Just start building and executing. Don't focus too much on building a business plan. Everything will change anyway so focus more on getting your product out there and get some feedback! These learnings are a thousand times more valuable and helpful to you understanding the value that your product brings to the end users. The mental gap is way bigger than the actual gap, but as soon as you're going, you realize it's much easier and fun than you may have thought it would ever be. *- Nicolai Watzenig – Co-founder & CEO, Birdback (Springboard)*

I wouldn't write a business plan until I had a product launched (even if minimal), some initial users, ideally paying, and confidence that the business model itself could be big enough to achieve whatever goals I had for the business. Come to think of it, I'm not sure I would ever write a business plan. *- Ray Grieselhuber – Co-founder & CEO, Ginzametrics (Y Combinator)*

We didn't have a formal business plan, but we did do a lot of planning. We always live by George Patton's famous quote: 'A good plan implemented today is better than a perfect plan implemented tomorrow.' If you're planning, just make sure it doesn't get in the way of taking action – always stay in motion. *- Ebrahimi – Co-founder & CEO, ReadyForZero (Y Combinator)*

Don't stress about the details. You don't know what you don't know, so stop making them up. Just write down a rough plan and go do it. Don't get stuck behind your computer trying to imagine the scenarios, because your imagination stinks. Stay behind the computer only as long as you are building something to put in front of customers. The key is to always find a way to exert yourself in the real world through your product. That's how you learn what you don't know about the world and validate whatever plan it is you've come up with. *- Rickey Yean – Co-founder & CEO, Crowdbooster (Y Combinator)*

We never wrote a business plan for any of the companies we ever founded, nor do I think I know anyone in Y Combinator who wrote a business plan before they got there. Now it's all about traction,

'A good plan implemented today is better  than a perfect plan implemented tomorrow.'

*– George Patton*

*'Entrepreneurship is the pursuit of opportunity without regard to resources currently controlled.'*

-Professor Howard Stevenson

users, revenue, and growth. Business plans are a relic of the past. *- Dan Siroker – Co-founder, Optimizely (Y Combinator)*

'Make something people want.' *– Y Combinator mantra*

What's a business plan? Kidding ... sort of. I think a business plan can take many shapes and forms, but in the early stages of a company I think the important parts to think about are the product, growth, and monetization, in that order. Whether that evolves into a 'business plan' or not is up to you.

The Y Combinator mantra is 'make something people want' and I really stand by those words because if you don't have a good product, you have absolutely nothing. The next part of the equation is getting people to use what you've built. And guess what? It makes it a hell of a lot easier to do that if you've built something great, but you still need to have a plan of attack. Don't just assume people will flock to you without putting out some breadcrumbs to lead them there. And then, finally, how are you going to pay the bills? In the early stages of a company, I don't think this is the most important problem to solve, but I do think there has to be a solid answer to the question. Later on in the life of a company, I think these three things start to equalize with each other, but in the beginning there's a clear priority. *- James Fong – Co-founder, Listia (Y Combinator)*

First, keep in mind that a business plan for a startup is very different from a business plan for an established company. You won't have detailed revenue and cost projections for three or more years. Instead, focus on the next twelve months. Figure out some basic facts: how much money do we need at a bare minimum? What's the soonest we can release something? Where does our product need to be to start making money? And outline a few scenarios: what will we do if we don't raise money? What if we raise a seed round? How would hiring one employee affect our costs? How would it affect our development time? Above all, remember that your business plan is just a starting point. It's going to change, sometimes dramatically. The process of thinking through the business plan is much more valuable than the plan itself. If someone's asked to see your business plan, they'll understand this. They're expecting it to just be a guess; you should make sure it's a thoroughly educated one. If this is a potential employee or investor, they want to know that you've thought through things as much as possible with the limited information you have. *- Ben Lerner – CEO, DataNitro (Y Combinator)*

Don't overthink the business plan. Opening Excel and spending a month building financial models with detailed projections might impress some investors, but won't actually make your business successful. Besides, most seasoned investors and entrepreneurs know that most assumptions fail and most metrics will have to be changed.

Instead, focus your business plan on truly understanding the market and even getting a few testimonials about your product or idea. A business plan containing quotes from potential customers or testimonials around an early-stage product is much more exciting than a theoretical argument around your business' potential growth rate.

As with your own business, approach the business plan with the 'product-market fit' mentality. Show a product idea and a market willing to pay for it; the other details will then flow naturally *- Wojciech Gryc – Co-founder & CEO, Canopy Labs (Y Combinator)*

I'm not sure the traditional 100-page business plans are as relevant now, especially if you want to start a software business. Since things change so fast when you start a business, whatever plan you write will be quickly outdated, and you're better off spending the time preparing yourself to eventually scrap the plan. I think it's worth putting together a four to five-page executive summary on key questions on your competitors, core differentiation, monetization, user acquisition, etc. (Incidentally, I think the YC application is a great place to start, even if you don't apply for the program. The questions are excellent forcing functions to cover these grounds (news.Y Combinator.com/apply).) You can also use the executive summary as homework to prep for discussions with potential investors, advisors and other entrepreneurs. Beyond that, just know whatever plan you write up, it'll change, and just be ready for it. *- Yu-Kuan Lin – Co-founder, Everyday.me (Y Combinator)*

Build something first. Validate that people want it. Then worry about the long-term game plan. There's no use in planning if you don't have a shred of evidence that people want what you're making. *- Ilya Sukhar – Co-founder & CEO, Parse (Y Combinator)*

1. Don't think about it, do it! It is your bible! It is so much more than a fundraising tool. It is essential to any idea; to test whether the idea is a valid proposition commercially, to chart progress and many other things. Importantly, treat it not as a static document, rather as something organic that grows with you and your company.
2. Write a clear and succinct executive summary that outlines your business proposition and USP. This is what ensures investors continue reading.
3. Research. Research. Research.
4. Be realistic, i.e. don't underestimate or exaggerate, it's the quickest sure-fire way for us to lose interest. *- Maila Reeves – Director of*

*Strategic Relationships & PR, ProFinda.com*

Nowadays business plans are one of the most misunderstood processes. The general advice is you should not write one. Instead you should do an A-B iterative search for a business. But I think it's the wrong lesson. I agree that writing a business plan for the sake of doing one is the wrong approach, but so is just blindly trying things out and seeing what works. The best companies, the one's that really have a big impact, are not a product of chance and luck. I'd say, give yourself three to five months to start the company you want. Research your market and your competitors. Make sure what you aim to build is not incrementally better, but really changes the market you are entering. Make sure the market is big enough, but not too big. Make sure you have a good enough team or you can leverage your network to build one that could solve this problem. Make sure it is a problem. If you build a business plan or not is not important – but a deep knowledge of your space, the market, what your product will solve and who you are going to solve it with is. Finally, don't seek approval; you can't just ask people what they think of your idea and expect valuable answers. If everyone agrees with you, dump the idea. If everyone disagrees with you then you might be crazy or you might be onto something. *- Daniel Palacio – Founder, Authy (Y Combinator)*

I don't think I've ever written a business plan in my life, at least not a proper or formal one, and it's been four years. I would advise a lot of planning with the flexibility to change and pivot as needed, but in the early stages going out and talking to potential users is far more important than trying to put together a large Word document. The closest thing I've done to crafting a business plan might be a loose set of pitch decks to potential partners and briefings we've written to the press. *- Lee Lin – Co-founder, RentHop (Y Combinator)*

Substance over symbolism. Your first business plan doesn't have to be of any certain length, look, font, etc.

In fact, I recommend you start by playing with your business idea using Post-its, markers and business model canvas, then creating your first 'ten-slide' deck. If you have done the first two steps properly, recording it as a formal business plan is easy. **- Yrjö Ojasaar, – Co-founder & CEO, publification (Springboard)**

Don't start by writing it. Sketch up the concept or make a prototype and discuss that with people that know the industry, then write a one-pager based on that, and prepare a pitch deck. That's all you need in the beginning to get going.

Most important things you should consider:

1. Have a market that is attractive enough for investors to invest in.
2. Know the industry.
3. Show that you have the team and skills to do it, and all you need is money.
4. Make sure that you can actually execute what you are pitching.
**- Sune Alstrup Johansen – Co-founder & CEO, The Eye Tribe (SUBC)**

The Eye Tribe

Writing an x-paged business plan should be one of the last steps for setting up your business. Your first steps should be to identify a problem, validate that it really exists, think about a great solution and talk to other people about the things you've come up with. Ignore people who say you

should be as secretive with your business idea as possible because it's all about execution in the end.

Only when you know that you're onto something real, you can start drafting a business model canvas and think about how your stream of revenue might look like and how you'd like to set up your company. Sometimes – and to be honest, I haven't come across a startup the following statement doesn't apply to – a business model canvas is more than enough. As your plans definitely will change while you're working on your project, planning it in detail before you've even started working on it may be a waste of your time. **- Oliver Lukesch – Co-founder & CEO, Weavly (SUBC)**

A business plan is a great way to go through the vetting process for an idea and help you work through some building blocks for strategy and execution. It's critical, but it's not a be-all-end-all. You won't replicate the plan exactly and you won't be able to predict the future with 100% certainty. So, do the exercise, but then do the work on your business.

Also, if you do a plan for capital raising, know that every person will have criticism on how it can be better. It has to be good enough, but eventually you need to stop working on it. Also, the more you can do to achieve real milestones in your business, the less important the plan will be. **- Carol Roth – media pundit and best selling author of The Entrepreneur Equation**

A popular answer to this is 'just do it', but everyone's not cut out to be an entrepreneur. Most successful businesses end up there after a harrowing roller coaster ride along the way. And most businesses that fail do so because the founder gives up. So it's worth thoughtfully considering whether this course is right for you.

A definition of entrepreneurship that I like is: 'the pursuit of opportunity without regard to resources currently controlled' – Professor Howard Stevenson

> *'If everyone agrees with you, dump the idea. If everyone disagrees with you then you might be crazy or you might be onto something.'*

(1983). I would add to this that success requires powerful intent and an unshakeable commitment to your vision of the future, not to a specific set of product features or revenue number, but to managing risks, adapting and making the business successful, and persisting despite naysayers, setbacks, and unexpected hurdles.

If you believe in the idea and that you're the right person to lead it, take the plunge, but don't spend excessive time on the business plan. Do spend some time thinking about each section of a typical plan. Think about what the keys to success will be in each area, actions required, and who/how you will accomplish them. Simply taking the time to do this will set you on the right path and align your team's priorities. But, time spent refining estimates and plans has diminishing returns at this stage when so much remains unknown.

It should also be a working plan, designed to be consulted, questioned, and revised regularly when things change or new information is discovered. Don't file it away and forget about it or you'll lose half its value. **- Lynley Sides – Co-founder & CEO, The Glue Network (Springboard Enterprises accelerator)**

When writing a business plan, just make sure you know that it will need to be fluid. We used the Lean Canvas and wrote our first plan in fifteen minutes. From then on, it's all about testing your riskiest assumptions from that plan, and adapting as necessary. Don't get stuck to a written plan if the market is telling you something different. **- Mikael Cho – Co-founder & CEO, ooomf (FounderFuel)**

> *'Almost every assumption you make in your business plan is going to be wrong.'*

Keep it under ten pages and don't spend too much time on it. Business plans are important to help people crystallize their thoughts, but once you actually launch the business you'll probably never look at the plan again. Almost every assumption you make in your business plan is going to be wrong, so being agile and listening to your customers will serve you better in the long run than a super-duper business plan. **- Ethan Austin – Founder & CEO, GiveForward (Excelerate Labs)**

Business plans are good. But don't spend too much time on this. Just do it. Get a prototype up. Get some users. Try, fail, repeat.

Selling is one of the most important things in any startup. As an engineer by training, sales is one of the last things I wanted to do after graduation. But I quickly learned that sales is what drives a company. And many of the shots are called by sales. Absolutely, sales is the #1 priority for 71lbs. We are constantly refining our customer

Melissa Gonzales

*'Don't under-estimate the power of a plan, but also know it's a roadmap and in year one you must be nimble.'*

acquisition and looking at expanding more customer acquisition programs. So my #1 point is: concentrate on selling, and your business model and plan will grow out of your selling experiences. **- Jose Li–founder & CEO, 71lbs (Excelerate Labs)**

Don't do it. A twenty-page business plan is useless for a startup; if you must write something, write a one or two page executive summary. Any business plan you write as a startup will be out of date before the first few pages have been written. Save yourself a ton of wasted time writing a useless document and, instead, invest all of your energy in testing the underpinning hypotheses implicit to the success of your proposed venture. Do this by talking to as many potential customers as possible. Aspiring entrepreneurs should also read Steven Blank's *The Start Up Owner's Manual* – the advice and lessons are priceless. **- David LaBorde – Founder, SwiftPayMD (Flashpoint)**

Don't underestimate the power of a plan, but also know it's a roadmap and in year one you must be nimble. It feels exciting and it's easy to dive into an idea without thinking it through, but make sure you are clear of your mission and the problem your company is solving. Then be ready to adjust your tactics along the way as you learn. **- Melissa Gonzalez-Caputo – Founder & CEO, Lion'esque Style (First Growth Venture Network)**

Don't write a business plan – at least not at the beginning. You're a startup, not an established business, so writing a business plan doesn't make any sense unless you've evaluated your business model. Complete a business model canvas, hit the pavement and verify every element of the canvas through interviews with prospective customers. I wrote what I called a 'business plan outline' to convince myself that the idea was doable, and that was a sketch of the problem, the value propositions, a list of possible partners and competitors, a rough set of initial milestones, costs and expected revenues. Now that I've written both, the Canvas is a better idea. - *Howard H. Hamilton – Founder & CEO, Soccermetrics (Flashpoint)*

Just do it! Your business plan will change a thousand times before it's right. The hardest thing to do is to start the first draft. The second is to let go of ideas. So often entrepreneurs get emotionally attached to an idea or a way of doing something. Keep the fundamental guts of your idea and let everything else be replaceable – remember this is a race, so anything that can give you an advantage, take, and go with it. - *Daniel Noble – Founder, Wooboard (Pollenizer)*

A business plan can be anything you want it to be. Too many entrepreneurs get paralyzed at the thought of writing a business plan. There is no law that says a business plan has to be twenty pages of closely written typescript with lots of Excel spreadsheets. And if you are talking to potential investors who think there is – find new potential investors. I speak to so many entrepreneurs who waste huge amounts of time drafting and re-drafting business plans and investor decks to fit 'what investors want to hear'. I speak to entrepreneurs who end up 're-concepting' their startup to be 'what investors want to hear'. If you can lay out, simply and compellingly, on one sheet of paper, exactly what your product is and how you plan to make money – that's a business plan. If you feel confident you can start a business and begin making money from day one based on the business model you've designed – that's a business plan. That's enough for you and any investor who is the kind of investor you want to work with. As Mike Tyson said, 'Everybody has a plan until they get punched in the face.' Focus on rolling with the punches – because there will be plenty of them – not endlessly drafting and re-drafting business plans. - *Cindy Gallop – Founder, IfWeRanTheWorld*

Business plans have drastically evolved in the past few years, especially in the startup space. Web and mobile-based companies are developing products before thinking through some of the key problems. A strong revenue model (or any revenue model at all) is one thing a lot of companies aren't thinking through. I think it's really important to have a loose idea about how you are planning to generate revenue and how to pivot on that idea if it doesn't work out.

I am speaking from a web-based startup standpoint, but for us a project roadmap was more important then a business plan in this first stage of our company. Map out the major milestones, timelines, potential problems and delays, and what you hope to learn in each phase of the development process.

Another huge change is the move from a detailed and structured business plan to an MVP and pitch decks. You have thirty seconds to sell your idea, so will it be easier to sell if people have the product in their hands or if they have to read through a twenty-page subjective document? I think business plans are often drafted at the wrong stage in the company's lifecycle. This is not to say that you shouldn't have a rough draft sketched out from the beginning so that there is a path to follow, but know that this will change drastically. At the stage our company is at, building an MVP and a pitch deck was far more valuable than spending weeks on a detailed business plan. I know the stage will come, but in the beginning take time to validate your idea. Prove your concept, give something to your user that is tangible, make it easy to understand, and then build your plan around that. - *Vanessa Dawson – Founder, Evry*

Write everything down. Write down the wildest, dreamiest concept of your business. This will serve as your best-case scenario. When things get muddled as you plan ahead – say six months or even a year later – you can always look back at what your original intention was in starting your

'Everybody has a plan until they get punched in the face.'

-Mike Tyson

company. If you and your partners disagree about a business decision, you can always go back and read the business plan to clarify things. Your business plan will also show phases or steps on how to get to your final concept. Use it as a guide on what to prioritize and when.

The process of writing down our business plan for POPVOX took us months to do. We wrote and re-wrote until we understood our vision. And we had fun too: we spent every weekend one summer sitting on the roof deck of Marci's apartment with our laptops. We even went out to the Bay Area, where my parents live, and did a big re-write sitting in their backyard. It's not quite a Bay Area garage Startup story, but we were able to enjoy the California sunshine!

Once you do have your business plan written down, don't be afraid to change it as you go along. Sometimes plans change. An even better idea may come along, or you might have to pivot because one concept didn't work. That's okay too. Just make sure you put it on paper. *- Marci Harris and Rachna Choudhry – founding team, POPVOX*

It will change. The static, thick business plan is a thing of the past; in today's dynamic world of LEAN learning and agility, the best thing you can do is have a clear strategy and the ability to learn and adapt quickly. This means you should be lean on the 'plan' and firm on the strategy and mission. *- Diane Tate – Manager, Mozilla WebFWD accelerator program*

If someone told me they were thinking about writing a business plan, I'd tell them to get a job or go back to school and forget the idea. Business plans are a total waste of time, and 'thinking about' signals you're just not ready. My chapter 'Quit Your Startup' in *Do More Faster* explains why. To start a company you need a freight train's momentum to destroy every risk that pops up in your path. This is why they say ideas are useless and execution is everything. Execution is the person in the room who walks right over and starts

hacking at the thermostat, even as everyone else in the room has the same 'great idea' that it's just too cold in there. *- Laura Fitton – Founder, oneforty, and author of Twitter for Dummies. Currently Inbound Marketing Evangelist at HubSpot.*

Stop planning and get started. It's easy to get bogged down in the details of your potential company – operations, a logo, a detailed business model. In reality, nearly all of your assumptions will be wrong, but you have to get out there with your vendors and customers to discover what is right. So put the notebook down and go talk to some customers! *- Alex Tryon – Founder & CEO, Artsicle*

Alex Tryon

Don't write it. Just do it! Business plans change regularly and the only reason you need one is when you are pitching to investors or if you are one of those people who brainstorms by getting the entire thing on paper, and even in those cases they just want to understand what you do as fast as possible, so typically you would put together a short and sweet PowerPoint. I do think it's important to put some things on paper, but don't waste time writing an in-depth business plan, just get started! *- Jesse Draper – Founder & Host, The Valley Girl Show*

Think the details through, but not that much! I have re-written my business plan four or five times. It is always changing and evolving, and if you spend too much time in your home office writing the business plan, someone else out there will be hitting the market with your idea. Go to market quickly and smartly!

Perhaps it was my background as a lawyer, but when I first set out to write my business plan, it had every detail and was over fifty pages. I had attended a seminar at my local library and they had given us a template that included everything but the kitchen sink, so to speak.

I wouldn't say the exercise was a waste of time, as it did get me thinking of every aspect of my business – from product development and sourcing to channels of distribution, pricing, financial projections, capital requirements, target customer and so on. When I wrote my first draft, I had a business plan 'expert' review it, and she had no comments except that she wanted to see product shots!

At the end of the day, I guess my advice to anyone writing a business plan would be to spend a lot of time researching your idea – that is the important part of writing a business plan. Make sure there is a need for what you are doing: who is your customer? Where should you sell? What kind of numbers can you expect immediately, in the short term and in the longer term?

Spend a lot of time on the financials in the business plan. Also spend a lot of time on the executive summary part of the business plan – everyone reads that – and that is what excites people. As for the rest – it is good to have, but don't be surprised if it becomes out of date very quickly. Be prepared for it to gather dust in your drawer as you forge ahead with the practical aspects of your business. *- Jacqueline Dinsmore – Co-founder & CEO, Luvali*

First and foremost, don't waste too much time writing a lengthy business plan. BUT make sure to think through all the key areas of your business before you embark on building it. Think about the market opportunity, competition, point of differentiation, revenue and monetization strategy, and your cost base, etc. These are important questions you must ask yourself and be comfortable with before you start moving ahead. How you get to those answers and how you document them in my opinion is not important. But having the answers and knowing the overall business strategy is critical. *- Sonia Kapadia – Founder & CEO, Taste Savant*

Before you build the plan make sure you are creating a solution to a real problem! I encourage spending a good amount of time doing a feasibility analysis before building the plan. This time should be spent investigating the industry, getting to know the key players (literally meet them in person), influencers, and the nuances of the industry. Focus on the problem you are trying to solve and really dive into the root of the problem. *- Kellee Khalil – Founder & CEO, Lover.ly*

Don't overthink it! Your business will shift off your business plan more than you could ever imagine (and that is okay). I would recommend being realistic with your budget, to give yourself enough working capital to stay in business while your plan gains momentum. Budgeting/paying very much for advertising early on in your business now, in the age of social media, would also be foolish. Trust your gut and don't spend too much time analyzing your business plan. *- Kyle Smitley – Founder & CEO, barley & birch*

When writing a business plan, any entrepreneur needs to be open to change. The business plan that we initially started out with had changed tremendously. With new technologies and the new wants and needs of our users, we have been forced to either add on or take away from what we started with. What I have learned is that if you fail at something, you can't keep trying the same thing over and expect a different result. You need to try something new and that is where success comes from. **- Juliette Brindak – CEO, Miss O and Friends**

The advice I offer on writing a business plan is to consider it a route map, helping you move from where you are now to where you want to be. Keep it brief (four to five pages) and include these key points:

I – what's the Idea for your business?
M – who is the Market you're going to serve?
O – what Operations do you need to get started?
F – are the Finances in order so sales exceed costs and, if not, how much funding is required?
F – which Friends will constitute your support network: a mentor, management team, industry experts, etc?

As you can see, it spells 'I'M OFF', and with this in hand you will be! **- Emma Jones – Founder, Enterprise Nation**

Don't bother! Big bulky business plans (the type that the banks like to see) can only accurately be written once you've gained insight and understanding of your market and your position within it. They can take months to produce properly. As soon as you start your business you'll quickly find yourself off script as the reality of your mission follows a course of action quite different to the optimistic outlook you described in your plan. In my personal opinion, and especially in the early days of a new business, you are much better off having a vision of where you ultimately want to go and then breaking this back into measurable and achievable goals which may be reviewed on a month-to-month, week-to-week basis. Manage your cash and control its flow. Understand your clients' needs and identify how to attract more of them. Build your product portfolio in line with

their requirements and then consider planning your future as you systemize, optimize and grow your operations. **- Celia Gates – Founder, The Observatory**

You hear a lot of mixed stuff about business plans. In the tech startup world, I think they aren't 100% necessary. That being said, I think it's very valuable to go through the process of writing one as a founder. It helps you articulate what you're doing and really solidify your message and plan. **- Bradley Joyce – Founder & CEO, Socialyzer (Tech Wildcatters)**

Do what is most beneficial and appropriate for you. For me personally, a design and a layout was far better at telling a story and a vision than any sort of written business plan. To this day, the guiding vision of Scan usually begins with a design that we build off of and work towards. **- Garrett Gee – Co-founder, Scan.me (KickLabs)**

*'"Do nothing" is an alternative to using your service.'*

Before starting a business plan, start writing stories about how your product/service makes your customer's situation better. Keep in mind that 'do nothing' is an alternative to using your service. Ask yourself: is using my service better than doing nothing? This framework of thought will be helpful in making key decisions along the way. **- Afifa Siddiqui – Co-founder & COO, Careerleaf**

If it's about technology, pause on the business plan. The barrier to entry is rather low in technology; just make a prototype and run some tests. See if you're building something people want. That's the only real test.

There's a time and a place for a business plan, but I belong to the school of thought that

> *'When you're so close to everything coming into view, it's easy to assume that it's all important, and you can end up wasting a lot of time on irrelevant, time-consuming number crunching, and extrapolation.'*

doesn't believe they are essential at the startup stage because we're much more product focused. I believe business plans create a great exercise when you're ready to optimize and scale, but end up doing little when you're just starting off. **- Hany Rashwan – Founder & CEO, Ribbon (AngelPad)**

All entrepreneurs will need to have a plan to show but, honestly, few investors will read the whole thing. Nail a one-page introduction to your company. Have strong financial information about the market for your products and your potential. Get your products into the right stores, so you have credibility. Utilize information about other companies in the market, their value and history. Potential investors will want to see proof of concept, so keep moving forward. Do not rely or wait on anyone else to move your business forward, this includes investors. I believe the main difference between success and failure for entrepreneurs is perseverance. A good investor will invest in you, not simply the idea. You must show what you are capable of achieving – often on your own. **- Jaclyn Sharp – Founder, fashion brand Imposter**

Keep it loose. It's much easier to report off of real data than to try and fabricate expectations or projections. Focus on generating the data you need, rather than dressing up data that's incomplete, irrelevant or unsubstantial.

The hardest part is distilling what you have into what you need. If you figure that the pieces of data you collect can be put into ten categories on a Y-axis, and you are discriminating it by ten variables on an X-axis, that's 100 data points you need to consider and evaluate. In reality, only three of the variables might really matter for the outcomes you need to show.

When you're so close to everything coming into view, it's easy to assume that it's all important, and you can end up wasting a lot of time on irrelevant, time-consuming number crunching, and extrapolation. The more focused you are on the data you need, the better the data will be. Get help from the outside: usually people with distance from the project are in a better position to point out the strongest, weakest and most critical elements to focus on.

As a point of reference, we've had seven versions of four different documents in the past nine months: our pitch deck, business plan, investor deck, and financial model. **- Mike Salter – Co-founder & Creative Director, We Are Pop Up (Springboard)**

Know that everything will generally take twice as long as you think it will and plan contingencies accordingly. For us, building a business plan was an iterative process because we had so many moving parts with insurance-specific problems like licensing delays, to the regular problems like customer acquisition costs. Also, there's no substitute to solving the battle of customer lifetime value versus acquisition costs by running a few tests. *- Jason Traff – Co-founder, Leaky (500 Startups)*

Stop! Don't write one. At least not the kind that you are probably imagining. Go download a free copy of Steven Blank's *Business Model Canvas* and give your concept some definition that way. Talk to some potential customers and get feedback. Do some wireframing (prototyping). Find a co-founder and build something. Learn. If you're risk averse, think about how risky it is to presume knowledge before validating your base assumptions.

Of course, there will always be exceptions, particularly if your idea requires capitalization right out of the gates, but don't underestimate the value of early data points, moving quickly and, most importantly, 'getting started'. *- Ken Johnson – Co-founder, Manpacks (500 Startups)*

Skip it. Just kidding. Writing a plan simply helps to make sure you have at least thought through most things. It helps avoid some of the problems that you may not have thought about. For example, if your product relies on the Facebook Ads API and they only give it away to large companies, then you need to think about a way to get around that problem first. Realistically you adjust every day and what you end up with rarely looks like what you envisioned from the start. *Rob Lenderman – Co-founder & CIO, and David Greenbaum – Co-founder & CEO, BoostCTR (500 Startups)*

Ha, don't do it? Well, I take it back. Early on, it's worth planning one or two intense thinking days where you can sit down and write out every single piece of your business model, strategy and plan for execution in a huge sprawling document. Articulate all of the brilliant insights, giant gaping holes you can't answer, all of the assumptions you're setting out to prove and then ... put it in a drawer. No one wants to read that.

After all that, find a way to shrink it all down to a simple product, a ten second explanation and then go get absolutely buried in feedback. *- Jay Lee – Co-founder & CEO, Smallknot (Techstars)*

The first piece of advice would be to do some initial validation on the idea before jumping head first into the business plan. And talking to friends and family doesn't necessarily count - talk to the people who you believe will be your actual target customers. When writing the business plan itself, be sure you can clearly articulate a real pain in the market and how your product's approach to solving that pain is not only better, but also clearly differentiated, from the existing products.

Next would be to start thinking early about how to build the best team possible. And absolutely do not settle for mediocrity. An outstanding person is at least ten times more valuable than a great person, and a great person is at least ten times more effective than a good one. So choose wisely because these are the people with whom you'll be experiencing some of the highest highs and the lowest lows over the coming years, and who will likely make or break your company's success. *- Karl Sun – Co-founder & CEO, and Ben Dilts – Co-founder & CTO, Lucidchart (500 Startups)*

If the pain point you are addressing in your business plan is one you have directly experienced, it will be a lot easier to build your plan and sell your vision. Building a business around something you can't relate to will be difficult. Although this seems obvious, sometimes I hear entrepreneurs pitch their ideas and there is no personal connection. I don't want you to sell me something I can buy on a shelf. Sell me something you've designed specifically with me in mind because you know what I'm going through. Then maybe I'll pull out my wallet. *- Maxine Manafy – Co-founder & CEO, Bunndle (500 Startups)*

Figure out what the most critical assumption is that you're making. The one that, if it turns out to be false, completely torpedoes your startup idea. Then figure out the quickest, cheapest way to test that assumption so you can start populating your business plan with real data, not assumptions. **- Bernie Yoo – Co-founder, Bombfell (500 Startups)**

The Bombfell Team

To the extent I put together business plans and models, I found them most helpful as an exercise in checking the assumptions behind our vision. A lot of entrepreneurs can't help but charge headlong into a project they feel excited about, so a business plan can be helpful in making sure there's a process in place that gets you from point A to B. Chances are, in putting the document together, you'll discover things you never really thought through. Don't stress about that or bullshit over it – it's totally normal – and instead just be aware of the parts of your business you still need to learn more about. Finally, don't overcomplicate the process with complex graphs and calculations any more than necessary – since it's mostly an exercise for your own benefit, keeping things clear and simple make the insights you'll arrive at easier. **- Adam Bonnifield – Co-founder, Spinnakr (500 Startups)**

Keep things simple. Articulate a clear value proposition and explain why you are uniquely positioned to execute on it. Focus on building products that have real-world value. Ask yourself this question: 'If my service were turned off in the middle of the night, what would my users do?' Think about what happens when Google goes down or Twitter goes down – their users care A

LOT. Those services are essential to their lives and that is the kind of company you want to build. **- Nirav Tolia – Founder & CEO, Nextdoor**

It's important to write a business plan early on, even if you don't show it to anyone else at first. It helps to shape the overall vision for your product and answer questions about market size. Just make sure you're still working on the product while you write the plan, and accept that you will need to make changes to it as your business evolves. **- Katrina Brickner – Co-founder, Marquee (Techstar)**

Don't write a business plan. Seriously. If you've got an idea for a product, try to figure out if someone will use it and if someone will pay for it. Talk to people who know the industry or who might be users. Then build it. The problem with a business plan is that, by the time you've finished writing it, your business will have changed. Instead, put together ten slides that show why someone should use or want to invest in your business. By the time you've finished putting that together, your business will have changed, but at least it didn't take you as long, and you can always re-use some of the slides later. **- Wink Jones – Co-founder & CEO, Mealticket (Techstars)**

Pick an enormous problem that has hurt you personally, then step away from your computer and find ten people with the same problem and talk to them about it for an hour each. If the problem is real, do your research and reach out to the five smartest people who have tackled it – whether they succeeded or not – and talk to them for ten minutes each. **- Nick Soman – Founder & CEO, LikeBright (Techstars)**

Don't write a business plan. These days a formal business plan is only useful to help organize your thoughts. Build, test, and constantly adjust a 'business model'. A startup is an experiment and there is just too much unknown to spend too much time writing down anything but questions. Talk to customers or prospects as soon as you have something to test.

Don't ask them for what features they want, instead observe them in their natural habitat dealing/struggling with the problem that you are trying to solve. Find ways to make their life easier by ironing out the inefficiencies. Steven Blank has lots of great material on this: 'no business plan survives first contact with customers.' And Steve Jobs always said that customers don't know what they want because they don't know what's possible. *- Vitaly Golomb – Founder & CEO, Keenprint (Funded by 500 Startups)*

Be realistic with your time, team, and vision. It is great to have a big vision, but you need to have the team and resources in place to be able to execute. Remain focused on the long-term vision, but flexible on the short-term execution of that vision. Your beachhead that gets you up and operational is likely to not be the same target market or business model that helps you reach profitability. *- Ryan Stoner – Founder & CEO, MoPix (500 Startups)*

Business plans are weird, right? The thing is that it's all bullshit, honestly. It's not a plan because it's going to change. I don't plan more than a starting point. A super-detailed business plan is not good for raising capital either – investors just don't have the time to go through them. A seven-slide deck is perfect, because you don't know all the details anyway. They just hope that you and your team have the aptitude and talent to pivot and adapt your idea as needed to evolve. Understand your starting point and stuff the projections. *- Jennifer Reuting – Founder & CEO, DocRun*

Start off with the biggest dream you can possibly have as idealistic as you possibly can. Don't limit your ambitions in your first business plan.

Then, after you've completed that business plan, put it in a drawer and forget about it, then write a new business plan.

Your second business plan will be about creating a business, rather than a dream. Focus more on the money-making aspect and keep your ideals in the back of your head, and try to make them as realistic as possible with the means you have.

Your business needs money for its survival, so don't write a business plan that has no plan for the money because it just won't work without that.

Always split up your business plan into phases and milestones, you simply cannot expect to go from point A where there is no business to point B where there is business; it requires many points along the way and you simply need to plan in a learning curve into your business plan or it just won't work.

A business plan is a key measure of readiness to start a business. As soon as you have a business plan that you personally feel contains all the information and all the thought that needs to go into starting a business, you should get started with the business. If you cannot write an entire business plan that leaves you feeling confident, you are not yet ready to start a business. *- Rogier Trimpe – Co-founder & CEO, VideoView*

Hold your horses! Take one step back. A business plan is a long list of assumptions about your business, on every level. Unless you validate these assumptions with your market, there's a 99% chance you will fail to execute the plan. Not because your planning was wrong, but because you didn't know what to plan. What do customers want? What do your users like? How much are they going to pay for it? These are key questions and you're not the one to answer them – your customers/users are.

A business plan is useful when you have validated the way you're going to make money/generate

users and your company is ready to scale. I highly recommend reading *The Lean Startup* by Eric Ries or *Running Lean* by Ash Maurya. You will thank me later. **- Cristian Andreica – Co-founder, Nexi (RockStart)**

Christian Andreica

Start with writing the press release you want at launch. It is a good way to focus on what is important to the success of the company, and who your target audience is. The most important part of a business plan is knowing the problem you solve and who your market is. Writing the press release clarifies that right up front.

Your first business plan is not going to be perfect, but it's a start and you just keep working at it. Ask someone that has written one before to help you write it or edit it so you can make changes and improve your plan. There are lots of online resources to check out and help you along the way. It's good to look over some actual business plans to get a feeling for what it should be like. **- Derek Dodge – Founder, 1Mind**

OMG. If someone told me they were going to write a business plan I would slap them! I think business plans take too long to write and I would rather them get out the building and talk to customers. Find out what people want, why they want it, and how much they want it. Before we did a single line of code for Happy Inspector, we spoke to twenty different customers and half of them were willing to pay for something we had not built. I'm not saying don't plan your business, but use better tools like Eric Ries' *Lean Startup*, Steven Blank's *Customer Development Methodology* or the *Business Model Canvas.* **- Jindou Lee – Founder,**

### Happy Inspector (StartMate and 500 Startups)

Writing a business plan to impress an investor may be the wrong approach. I'd say hold off on it. First, create an informative deck for your product along with a detailed financial plan. Those are the only pieces of collateral one needs to raise money at first. Contrary to what we had initially thought, the financial plan has really helped set our business straight. The business plan will come naturally through smart planning and confidence in the product. **- Sam Friedman – CEO, and Alex Israel – COO, ParkMe**

We wrote a sixty-page business plan, five-year financial model, and fifty-slide PowerPoint deck for the first iteration of NextBigSound. Those documents took hundreds of hours to pull together and no one ever looked at any of them. At the end of the day, a business plan is a story. It's a story about a team, an idea, and a future world where the business in question plays a critical role.

The exercise should focus on figuring out the best way to tell this story. If you are a designer, perhaps a highly visual ten-slide deck that you flip through on an iPad is the best way to tell the story. If you are a top-notch programmer, maybe an interactive site with an obscure link you can send to potential investors (or include in your email signature) is the best approach. If you're knowledgeable about the customers and the market you hope to serve, the best route could be to collect ten quotes from future potential clients with their photos on one page. The goal of this part of the process is to capture the investors' imaginations.

The rest of the time prior to investment is about them justifying their instinct. Some investors need in-depth financial models, some need complex market size estimates, and some need deep reference checks. I would obviously have rough sketches of these sorts of things, but caution against putting too much time into any of these 'traditional' business plan components as the

# 'The "pay for" part is crucial. Do price discovery as early as possible.'

time would be much better spent on getting your story right. **- Alex White, – Co-founder & CEO, NextBigSound (Techstars)**

Don't write a business plan. Instead, focus on the lean startup canvas, paying special attention to the customer need. Engage with potential customers early and often. Don't be afraid that they will say 'no'. At first, you will be hearing more 'no' than 'yes', which is good because this feedback will tell you what not to do. The goal is to continue refining your idea down to the minimum viable solution that a customer will pay for. The 'pay for' part is crucial. Do price discovery as early as possible because customers won't give you honest feedback until you introduce cost into the equation **- Justin DeLay – Co-founder, TempoDB (Techstars)**

Don't do it. Nobody reads a business plan. However, it is good to think through the big issues of your business such as: how does this business get to $1 million a year in revenue. Is that done easily? Is this market growing? Is there demand? What core issues am I solving for my customers?

There are different dynamics for people doing B2C Startups versus B2B. If you're doing B2B, you need more customer and revenue proof. You need to be able to think through your price point and you need some paying customers. If you're doing B2C, you have more freedom to be innovative with the product and the market, and while you don't need proof of revenue, you need proof of usage and engagement. **- Mike Lewis – Co-founder & president, Kapost (Techstars)**

Stop. Make a deck and/or an executive summary. Most traditional business plans require too much detail/foresight that you simply don't have at your early stage. If you have a strong team and you picked a big idea in a large market, you're better off keeping things at a high level early on. 'No battle plan survives contact with the enemy.' So start with a high-level strategy and quickly build something you can put in front of customers. Everything will change after that. **- Reece Pacheco – Co-founder & CEO, Shelby. tv (Techstars)**

Don't write one, they're a waste of time. I would, however, recommend filling out the Y Combinator application. Even if you don't submit it, it'll force you to really think through what you're doing.

Other than that, a one-page document with a paragraph of notes and some bullet points arranged haphazardly is probably just fine. There are a few good reasons why accelerator applications are so short. The obvious reason is because they are quicker to read and reviewers have a lot to get through. But more importantly, anything you write beyond guiding principles and fundamental assumptions is subject to swift and radical change. It is important to think through the market, your customers, competitors, etc., but '$X/year', 'people who do Y', and 'Z's W product' is probably sufficient for a first pass. You'll figure out the rest as you go. **- Steve Krenzel and Brandon Bloom – Co-founders, Thinkfuse (Techstars)**

The goal of a plan is to try to figure out the riskiest part of your business and de-risk it. We used a business canvas to breakdown business ideas very quickly and identify which part of the business we felt the most nervous about. Then, we got to work trying to de-risk that part of the business through either interviews, market research or, ideally, some kind of user test. For one early test we said we would continue the business if we could make substantial progress with a big company partner in the next 30 days. It was an arbitrary test over an arbitrary time period, but as we've done more, we've learned to have better instincts about what is real proof and what's a false signal. We encourage everyone to just get started talking to the market. *- Miro Kazakoff - Co-founder & CEO, and Tom Rose – Co-founder & CPO, Testive (Techstars)*

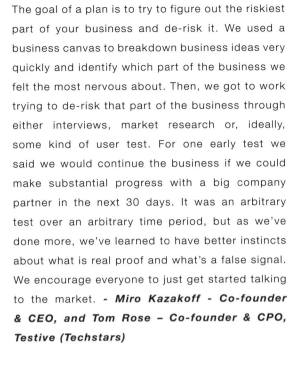

FUNDR

AISING

# FUNDRAISING

Early in 2010 was the first time that I attempted to raise funding for a venture. At the time, I was working on a custom footwear brand that, to date, had exclusively created one-off high-performance footwear for professional athletes. The athletes had once been big names, but were now in the twilight of their careers and no longer had a sponsor or were in-between sponsors. Our revenue model was very unique in that we had thrown the model of paying professional athletes to wear our footwear out the window and replaced it with a model that charged professional athletes for our design services and the use of our brand. The brand was showing light traction having produced footwear for both NBA (National Basketball Association) and MLB (Major League Baseball) players. Our goal was to take our core value and translate it into a mass-market line of footwear. To do this we decided that we needed to raise funding.

The first two people we pitched the company to were Dan Brestle, the former President and COO of Estée Lauder Companies and Board Member of Abercrombie & Fitch, and Neil Shapiro, Managing Director at a private equity fund that Dan was Senior Advisor to. I had gotten to know Dan during my time with Estée Lauder and Neil was a recent introduction.

We had done some things right. We had a relationship with Dan who knew the luxury business inside and out, although in a different vertical. Not only did Dan have financial means to invest in the company but would also make an incredible advisor. Also, Dan brought value contacts into our network, which included Neil Shapiro. But when it came to our presentation, the floorboards opened up and we fell through. We started off the pitch by proudly presenting them with our sixty-eight page, full-color business plan. The best way to get anyone to ignore you completely is to hand them something interesting to read. Luckily for us, the business plan wasn't that interesting so they both flipped through it very quickly, starting with the executive summary, then moving to the team for a second, then to the financials before placing it on their laps.

We were selling the idea of a spin-off brand called lūp (pronounced 'loop') that could be a high-end lifestyle line of footwear with subculture sporting influences. I started the presentation with a brief introduction to the company, what we had done, where we were at that time, and where we were going. Our team was very strong on the footwear design and manufacturing side, with my fellow co-founders Daniel Bailey and Omar Bailey (no relation) bringing a wealth of experience to the team. We wanted to talk about the team first because, as we were selling the future, we felt that it was important for Dan Brestle and Neil Shapiro to feel confident that, with their financial support, we were the right team to make the vision happen. It took me about three minutes to introduce myself; Daniel, sitting at the back of the room with a dollar slice from 2 Bros Pizza in his hand, took a little longer to introduce himself between mouthfuls. Omar was joining us via Skype as he was away visiting factories. Unfortunately, twenty minutes into Omar's introduction, as he started to discuss his fourth internship, we had run out of time and had to cut the presentation short. We also didn't have any samples of the new lūp line — just renders — nor any proof of customer demand for lūp. Rookie mistakes all round.

In the end we were not a fit for Neil's fund, but it was a great learning experience. A week after the presentation, Neil and I connected again. He helped me break down the presentation and provided us with a great base from which to move forward. Since then, lūp has grown as a brand, recently launching our second line of lifestyle footwear.

Our goal as entrepreneurs is not to raise funding, but to create a product or service that will become a real business. If you focus your efforts on gaining users, building a killer product, and establishing a creative team that can execute, the money will find you.

If the path to capitalizing your business requires raising money, you should:

1) Generate relationships with the right investors early, far before you need their funding. Our first investor in VineUp was Oxford International College and this came about due to a relationship that we had generated with them years in advance of the need for funding. We are edTech so they were the perfect organization to bring on-board.

2) When you do start to look to generate strategic relationships, be engaging and interesting. Try not to come across needy and, finally, don't become creepy or stalker-like. If your potential investors are not engaging, leave it for six months and try again. A simple thing to keep in mind is that the best relationships are those that are built on giving and not asking.

3) I know this is hard to do, but try as hard as you can to not fundraise when you need it. Just like your ex-girlfriend or ex-boyfriend, investors smell desperation and they will not go near you until you don't want them anymore.

4) If you don't have an existing relationship with the investor or fund, don't waste your time cold calling or emailing, do what you can to get an introduction from someone whose opinion carries weight with the fund managers.

In this section, founders share their thoughts on areas that entrepreneurs should focus on when fundraising.

Dan: You'll rarely hear 'no' from an investor because they'll usually either say yes right away because they're excited or they'll defer the decision until later. The things that will force an investor to make a decision now versus later are really important. Demo day for us was a forcing function where investors felt they could potentially miss out on a deal, which I think is really important to get them to decide one way or the other. The first check is always the hardest and once you have someone to lead the round it's really easy to get someone to invest. Hearing a 'yes' from investors is great. Hearing a 'no' is also great because it saves you time from having to pursue them further.

Pete: Because of our early traction and Paul Graham's help, we were in a very favorable situation where we had great introductions to investors who suddenly had to compete all at once. If an entrepreneur is not in that situation, one thing they can do is form early relationships with VCs while they're building out prototypes and getting their earliest customers. Keeping the VCs informed about how things are moving along will hopefully create a situation where they can find that first check early and try to start a competitive situation like we had.

Dan: One of the best times to raise money is when you don't need to. Investors can smell it if you're desperate to raise money and will be more reluctant to invest and give you good terms. You have a lot more leverage if you're in a position where you're not desperate for money because it makes investors scared that they're going to miss the deal and forces them to make a decision.
*- Pete Koomen and Dan Siroker – Co-founders, Optimizely (Y Combinator)*

*'Never pitch the first time you meet an investor.'*

1. Look to build real friendships and relationships with investors before you look to pitch to them.
2. Never pitch the first time you meet an investor. Instead, find something that you have in common to talk to them about; their blog post or something that you feel strongly about that is relevant. Show an interest in their interests.
3. Find the connectors. If you want to get a meeting with anyone you need a referral. Don't spend your time pitching at events or going to startup meetings. Instead, work on your prototype and find one or two key people that believe in you and ask them if they could make any introductions. These people can get the whole of Silicon Valley on your side. So as early as possible, finding those people that are connected that will talk you up and make the introductions that you need.
4. Get on Angel List, it's awesome!

My biggest piece of advice is to have a prototype. If you can't build a prototype, people will have a hard time believing in you.

When it comes to fundraising, there are several things that entrepreneurs should stay away from when pitching their company:

1. This might sound counter-intuitive, but if you have a little bit of revenue and traction, don't dig into it too much. You need to keep them focused on how you are going to change the world, and not metrics that can put restraints on their imagination.
2. Do not ever say, 'If we get just 1% of the market we will be making lots of money' ... particularly if it is China.
3. If a VC suggests that you make some changes to your direction, don't agree just to humor them. Have a real reason why you disagree and stand by it, but also be open to exploring their suggestions.
4. If you are raising money when you need money, you should really be concentrating more on selling your product. That is not the time to start raising capital. *- Jennifer Reuting – Founder & CEO, DocRun*

'People think great pitches are like a good novel, but actually it's just a punchline: "Knock Knock!" "Who's There?" "TRACTION."'

- Dave McClure

1. Remember, if VCs had enough motivation left then they'd be entrepreneurs. So, however badly you think you need a VC, they actually need you much more. This makes the negotiation process much less intimidating.

2. Pick a number, any number. Don't let VCs get away with valuing your life's work. Try to set your own price whenever you can. They'll always argue you down if they need to.

3. Don't take holidays. It's easier to negotiate on holidays. If there are none when you're trying to raise, make one up! Happy Schmelalala! *- Seth Priebatsch – Chief Ninja, LevelUp (DreamIt)*

## 'If you have a little bit of revenue and traction, don't dig into it too much.'

1. Know your stuff! All of it, most importantly your figures. Whilst financial projections are pure speculation, we still want to know that you understand your business inside out and have thought the details through thoroughly.

2. Don't be afraid of failure/rejection. Always ask for feedback as to why you were unsuccessful. Be polite even if you are rejected, you never know, with a few tweaks (or a pivot) we may change our minds and invest in you after all.

3. Prove your concept, secure some external investment (however small), get traction and revenue coming in and, importantly, have some skin in the game. If you aren't risking something yourself, why should we?

4. Choose and profile your proposed investor, do not use a scattergun approach.

5. WHAT, WHY, HOW, WHEN? For you and for me, respectively: What are YOU looking for? Why do you want it? (i.e., what are you going to do with my money?) How are you going to get there? When are you going to get there? Additionally, what do I get out of it (equity)? Why should I invest (ROI)? How long do you need the investment for? When do you need it? And, importantly, when and how is the exit envisioned? *- Maila Reeves – Director of Strategic Relationships & PR, ProFinda. com*

Maila Reeves

1. Find a person you admire and who inspires you to keep going when the going gets tough.

For me, this was Sheryl Sandberg, but I don't think it necessarily has to be someone famous or even in your industry. Sheryl was really important to me because I was fortunate enough to meet her at Facebook's headquarters in January 2011 before I started my company. She basically posed a question to all of us: 'What would you do for the next five years professionally if you knew everything in your personal life would work out?' If we all trusted our heart and our instincts and didn't feel the need to conform to societal or external pressures, what would we truly do? I knew, for me, it was beginning this venture and that I needed to do anything and everything to make sure that the company was well funded and had the right investors.

2. Find a really awesome partner who can keep the business running smoothly while you are out meeting with VCs and other investors.

First time founders should consider bringing in another person early on. This person can be a 'co-founder' or a rock solid no.2. Raising capital and running a company can get very lonely and it's a ton of work. There are many emotional twists and turns. Doing it alone makes it more difficult both professionally and personally to sustain a

# TOP 4 POINTS

## TRACTION
### IS KING

## KNOW
### YOUR STUFF

### GENERATE RELATIONSHIPS
## WITH INVESTORS
### EARLY

### HAVE A
## STRONG
### TEAM

business.

3. Unfortunately, genius will always be 1% inspiration and 99% perspiration. Recognize this before you raise capital and vest equity accordingly.

Sleep deprivation and sacrifice are both part of the adventure. Your family and friends won't appreciate your new 'missing-in-action' status, but it's your job to stay focused on the end goal. Expect long days, little vacation, and a limited social schedule. I don't think I worked harder in my life than when I was trying to get my company off the ground and raising capital. Make sure that your equity vests based on contributed effort and time, and that this is worked out prior to taking external investment. *- Danielle Weinblatt – CEO, Take the Interview (DreamIt)*

Read *Venture Deals* by Brad Feld. Get an outstanding attorney who has done dozens of venture financings, and rely on him/her heavily. Don't just optimize on valuation – understand that other terms, particularly liquidation preference, can be just as important.
*- Jack Groetzinger – Founder, SeatGeek (DreamIt)*

Raising capital is a big undertaking and I always tell first-time entrepreneurs to focus on WHO your first investors are and how they can provide strategic value. Many startups are often tempted to take as much money as possible too early in the company's development. I recommend taking a smaller amount of money from the right people who can mentor and help you in your earliest phase. Your angel investors are going to be your biggest fans and typically invest because they believe in YOU and want to help you succeed, so choose wisely. *- Kellee Khalil – founder & CEO, Lover.ly*

Develop a clear, concise, and compelling 'elevator pitch'. Be able to articulate what your problem and solution is in a few short sentences. For example: 'User A spends B time on C, which is problematic because D. The product we are building offers a better alternative because E. *- Brett Hellman – CEO, hall (AngelPad)*

In addition to networking like crazy, the best advice is to have a thick skin, expect a lot of rejection, and keep in mind that everyone you meet is someone you might end up going back to. Most of the investors in Ranker passed the first time I pitched them (it was at the nadir of the economic scare, and we were just starting to get traction), and came on board when I came back nine months later with a lot of traction. When you come back and show someone that you have done what you said you were going to do, you've instantly gotten over a lot of hurdles in getting an investor to write a cheque. *- Clark Benson – Founder & CEO, Ranker (LaunchPand LA)*

Don't put all your effort into fundraising, the further you get the product, user base, team, or the company ahead, the better chances you stand. I always hated the advice about being 'picky about your investors', because no one wanted to invest in the first place. How can you be picky in that situation? Being picky is a luxury that few startups get. However, eventually we were in the situation where we could choose between many top investors, and we are now extremely happy we ended up going with True Ventures. *- Chris Thür – Co-founder & CEO, Ovelin (Startup Sauna)*

Unless you're a serial entrepreneur with a notable success behind you, it's much easier to raise seed money from individuals in your network than from people you've just met. Our investors are all individuals that a Glue team member knows personally. It makes sense to focus your efforts on your immediate network first.

VCs are often willing to meet when it's too early for them to invest. These meetings can provide valuable two-way learning, but can also burn a lot of time, so be clear and realistic about the outcomes you expect, ask a lot of questions, and plan these selectively.

A compelling elevator pitch is essential as you never know when you may meet a potential investor. I described Glue to someone's father at my son's baseball game, not knowing he was a successful entrepreneur and investor, and he later invested in us.

A solid, well-practiced ten-slide (+/-) pitch is the must-have. A few specific appendix slides may be important for addressing likely questions. But forty pages of detail isn't needed or even meaningful at the seed stage. Instead, polish your short pitch by making sure your storyline is clear and compelling, your evidence and rationale airtight, assumptions believable, and your verbal presentation confident and polished. Seek out presentation outlines, feedback, and opportunities to pitch at events – either through an accelerator program, searching online, or asking your network. *- Lynley Sides – Co-founder & CEO, The Glue Network (Springboard Enterprises accelerator)*

There are three basic tips that we would give:

1. Build a great product in a compelling market.
2. Be able to show some initial traction.
3. Network for the right introduction.

The first two are pretty common these days, but traction seems to be more important for 500 Startups than for most seed funds. As far as I know, 500 Startups still does not have any application process. Rather, they rely on their mentors and other portfolio companies to recommend high-quality Startups and entrepreneurs that they have interacted with personally.

For example, there is a great company called IconFinder that we've actually integrated into Lucidchart to allow users to quickly find icons and images they can use in their diagrams.

Our interactions with the IconFinder team had always been positive, the product worked great for us, and we knew that they had quite a bit of traction. As a result, it was a no-brainer to put in a good word for them with 500 Startups when they started looking to raise some funding and we're glad they're now part of the 500 family.- *Karl Sun – Co-founder & CEO, and Ben Dilts – Co-founder & CTO, Lucidchart (500 Startups)*

*'Fundraising always takes two times the amount of time and is four times more difficult than you think it will be.'*

1. Put the time into building relationships; investors are much more comfortable saying 'yes' when they really know you and have seen you moving the business forward.

2. You have to be able to explain your what, why now, and why someone should care about your business in less than ten seconds. It takes a lot of iteration to really distill it.

3. Fundraising always takes two times the amount of time and is four times more difficult than you think it will be. *- Todd Silverstein – Co-founder & CEO, Vizify (Techstars)*

Todd Silverstein

The best advice is to put all your focus on the product, not the funding. If you concern yourself with trying to raise money at all times, this will distract you from achieving the work that needs to be done. Come up with an idea you can stand behind, and put the proper people in place to succeed.

Getting a VC to invest in your product is an amazing boost of confidence, but it shouldn't be the absolute be-all-end-all focus. Don't be distracted from the work. If you have the courage to see your vision through, and it's something unique and wonderful, there'll be no need to spend half your time trying secure funding. Investors will flock to you. *- Sam Friedman – CEO, and Alex Israel – COO, ParkMe*

Raise as much money as you can comfortably raise, but begin the process by asking for as little as you can possibly justify. We asked for $300k coming out of Techstars, but ultimately raised about triple that in our seed round. For our Series A we started off asking for $4 million, but ultimately raised $6.5 million. It is much easier to expand the round than to adjust downward if the demand isn't there.

If you are fortunate enough to have competing offers, first remember that is a great problem to have, and always optimize for the investor rather than the valuation. *- Alex White – Co-founder & CEO, NextBigSound (Techstars)*

*'You will be working with these people for a long time, so make sure that personalities and priorities are aligned.'*

Make sure that your early investors are aligned with your vision and founding team. At the earliest stages, strategies, plans, and products change rapidly while searching for product/market fit. Your investors should believe in where you are headed, and provide patience and support as you figure out how to get there. You will be working with these people for a long time, so make sure that personalities and priorities are aligned.

Do: raise from the most strategic investors possible, even if they don't come with the highest valuation.

Don't: let the fundraise drag on indefinitely. Set a deadline to drive action.

Do: establish a lead investor as early as possible. This person will be invaluable in filling out the round.

Don't: let fundraising consume you. Keep building the business in parallel. *- Justin DeLay – Cofounder, TempoDB (Techstars)*

Mike Lewis

I'm a big supporter of the 'lines not dots' theory (from Mark Suster). VC's are looking for companies that they know and have seen make progress. Even if you don't have much of a product or traction, you should still meet and get to know the VC's out there. You want to have second, third and fourth meetings with VC's, and those meetings to be reviewing the progress you've made. If you only start to go visit with VC's once you've made good progress, it's harder to build the relationship.
*- Mike Lewis – Co-founder & president, Kapost (Techstars)*

## 'Fundraising is a means to an end, not an end in and of itself.'

Do: meet investors as early as possible. Blog/tweet/engage in conversation with them online so you build your own presence. Time your fundraising well (avoid holidays/vacations), get everyone ready at the same time. 'Be genuine'. Think about your long-term reputation.

Don't: don't get upset at 'no'. Just say thanks and keep going! Don't pitch angel 'groups'. Don't forget that fundraising is a means to an end, not an end in and of itself. *- Reece Pacheco – Cofounder & CEO, Shelby.tv (Techstars)*

Raise as much angel money as you can, and make it last as long as humanly possible. There's a shortage of early-stage VC money (or rather, a surplus of angel-funded startups), which means most tartups who raise angel money won't be able to raise VC money. Treat your angel money as your first and only source of funding, and try to get to revenue-neutral as soon as possible, either through product if it's fairly simple technology, or through early-stage alpha product with customization and services if it's not. *- John De Goes – Founder & CEO, Precog (Techstars)*

Get a strong lead investor and have them do introductions for you to other investors. A warm introduction goes a long way.

Be selective about what investors you take money from. This is usually referred to as 'smart money'. Our investors often went to bat for us and helped out in dire situations. We were fortunate that we had an all-star team of investors. They were worth much more than the money that they gave us.

Do take smart money and that's not the same as 'do not take dumb money,' We had a few key investors that were invaluable far beyond their monetary contribution. That said, if anybody tells you that they are smart money, they are probably not. You'll recognize smart money because they will be providing value to you well before you sign a deal.

Do not underestimate how long a current or future round will take. Get started early! *- Steve Krenzel and Brandon Bloom – Co-founders, Thinkfuse (Techstars)*

First of all, tackle a big problem, one that can lead to a significant and positive impact on the lives of people. Second, find an angle that can get you some ways with relatively limited resources. Third, go to institutional investors once you have put together something tangible (a bright team and a first alpha or beta of a product), and you can justify clearly why this is a big opportunity and how the funds will be used to go after it. - *Erik Lumer – Founder, CircleMe*

*'The best introductions come from founders that the investor has already invested in.'*

Put together a list of at least 100 investors that you'd like to talk to. Categorize them and then figure out who the hell can introduce you. The best introductions come from founders that the investor has already invested in. Be prepared for a shitload of advice and rejection. Attempt to consolidate all of your meetings over a very compressed period of time. This communicates urgency, competition and momentum. As a bonus, by doing this, you'll also either close your round quicker or find out you're unfundable faster. *- Dana Severson – Co-founder & CEO, Chasm.io (AngelPad)*

# STARTUP REVOLUTION

## THE HUB FOR REVOLUTIONIZING THE WAY STARTUPS WORK

FB.COM/STARTUPREV

@STARTUPREV

STARTUP REVOLUTION

STARTUPREV.COM

**COMMUNITIES**
**LIFE**
**METRICS**
**BOARDS**
**CEO**

THE ACCE

PROG

EXPER

LERATOR

RAM

IENCE

# THE ACCELERATOR PROGRAM EXPERIENCE

One of the biggest challenges that startups face when participating in an accelerator is that they are not prepared for the intensity of the three months and struggle to adjust their priorities during the course of the program.

We recently shadowed a few companies through the Springboard London program. During the first two weeks of the program, each company had eighty meetings with mentors; this had a couple of effects. After the two weeks were over, they had figured out their core message for their company, developed a robust business model, increased their Rolodex exponentially, and lined up a host of meetings with potential partners. However, their operations suffered as they weren't left with much time free to work on product-development and sales. But once they got back to it at the beginning of the third week, they were rearing to go and found themselves working at a whole new level. This is a common trend among companies going through accelerators and it's something, with prior knowledge, they could have avoided. One solution would have been to hire up before the accelerator so the operations of the company go unhindered while the founders are occupied with mentor meetings. Another side effect of meeting so many qualified mentors is that they often each have different and opposing opinions to the same issue. Which super smart, super experienced mentors' advice do you follow? Neither. The suggestions they provide should be seen as data points and you need to process and weight them as such.

The typical middle of a program focuses on product development, testing, business development and traction. Because the companies work in the same space for most accelerators, it really forces all the founders to work together and work hard with little distraction. This provides them with an abundance of support through the other companies in the program, mentors and the programs management team. It also nurtures an environment that supports the tunnel vision that they need to iterate as quickly as possible.

The final section of an accelerator typically reverts back to a more intense mentoring format, focusing on fine tuning their pitch, generating early relationships with investors, and preparation for demo day. Demo day is where the accelerator graduates get the chance to showcase their companies through a live pitch to a room full of investors.

In every accelerator, the managers put on programming to teach the founders specific skill and content or to inspire them to work at their peak. Generally, there are three different types of programs. One is workshops (for example, "how to be a great CEO," "growth hacking," "business modeling," "financial modeling," etc). Second, they host speakers that talk about different subjects related to starting a company. And third, they bring in founders to share their founder stories and reminisce on their best or most successful experiences.

In this section, along with the short entries, we've selected a few startups to elaborate on their experiences of participating in an accelerator program.

# SENDGRID

**ISAAC SALDANA**, Founder
**TIM JENKINS**, Founder
**JOSE LOPEZ**, Founder

**Founded:** 2009
**Subscribers:** 200,000
**Funding raised:** $27.4 Million
**Accelerators:** Techstars Boulder (2010)

*Started by three engineers with frustrations over their transactional emails not getting delivered, SendGrid is a leader in the transactional email delivery market. (The emails that big companies like Facebook have to send out when you reset your password? That's transactional email.) SendGrid replaces your old email infrastructure so you don't have to build, scale, and maintain your email systems in-house. They've already been named one of the Top 16 OnDemand "Cloud Computing Private Companies to Watch."*

One of the things that really attracted me to Techstars is that it's a mentorship driven program. I knew that I needed help because I didn't know what I didn't know, and I didn't know what to look for and what to research. What's really interesting about Techstars is that they have overall mentorship for everyone, but they also have tailored mentorship to fit your need. In our case we were all technical founders, so they were able to help us with pricing, messaging, how to pitch, and how to talk about our products so that not just developers (our target market) can understand it but so can everyone else. The reason that was really important, and hard for us to understand initially, is because sometimes we'll meet a CEO at a conference, but they wouldn't always understand what we do so they don't talk to their CTO about our product. So if the CEO isn't technical and you're talking to them about something technical, you want that CEO to end up talking to their CTO about it. The only way to do that is for them to really understand your value proposition. That was interesting for us to learn – being perceived as valuable versus just focusing on our customers. From this we also realized there are people that can help you get customers, so having a pitch that everyone would understand was one of the things that we worked on during the program which was really helpful.

The facet of the program that really stood out to me was the customized mentorship and that the mentors were willing to help without expecting anything in return. That was really great to see. In fact now I really want to help entrepreneurs because of what I've been through at Techstars. I've heard of mentoring in exchange for getting a piece of a company, but in this case it was independent mentors being there to help and not expecting anything in return. One of the things that happened out of our experience was that not only were they our mentors during the Techstars program, but they became my lifetime mentors.

# CLOUDABILITY
**MAT ELLIS, Founder/CEO**

**Founded:** 2011
**Funding raised:** $9.8 Million
**Accelerators:** Techstars Cloud,
500 Startups, Portland Seed Fund
and Portland Incubator Experiment
(PIE).

*Cloudability is based in Portland, Oregon and is the financial management tool for monitoring and analyzing every cloud expense across any organization. The company has participated in four different accelerator programs.*

Techstars is one of four accelerator programs we participated in so we're a big fan of the whole idea. We participated in two in Portland (Portland Incubator Experiment & Portland Seed Fund), one in California (500 Startups), and one in Texas (Techstars Cloud). However, Techstars was the only program where we went through the entire accelerator program. What stood out about Techstars was the standard of mentors and how super focused they were. We were a bit skeptical going into Techstars because we weren't the typical "use case" for an accelerator program at the time since we already had funding, revenue, and 7 employees. More specifically, we were concerned what our investors would think when we told them we were going to go off to "school" for three months to run this business.

We went into the program with some trepidation but the mentors blew us away on our first day. Without offering any advice whatsoever, they challenged our pitch and what we were doing by immediately focusing on all the areas of our business that weren't well thought out. If we only sat with them and had them ask us questions, it would have been an amazing enough experience because when you do this 50 times, you end up compressing about 12-18 months of

deep strategic thinking into a smaller time frame. It's especially valuable because in these programs you have passionate founders who are engineers, product geeks, and designers – people who love to build things – but to give it some life and some wings you have to ACTUALLY figure out the business model.

A specific experience I can point to is that we always knew we would join cost and usage data together but our next step was seeing what we were going to do with all that. The continuous interrogation from mentors made us realize that we're not measuring cost or usage, but we're actually measuring the return, the ROI on cloud spending. From there we realized that the usage data is absolutely critical so we began to move the whole company for the next 8 months towards building out that part of the products because they had helped us realize it was so critical. Though we knew it in the back of our heads, it was made much more immediate and important when we were forced to explain to 50 very smart people why you're not doing it already.

Also, at the time, the idea that the cloud was going to consume the world was difficult to swallow, even for fan boys like us. But then you have a couple people who really understand what you're doing and who know without doubt that the trend is only going to continue. Then they take it a step further and tell you that you can be an absolutely critical part of that cloud trend because there's all this money moving into the cloud that needs to be managed and optimized. No one said to us "you're like a supply chain for cloud," but a couple of mentors came very close to saying that from just a half hour of speaking with us. This helped us to fundamentally crystallize our messaging; I don't think we would have raised the money we did without such a clear message about what we were doing.

I found the experience so valuable that if I went off to create another startup, I would certainly be applying for a position in the next class of Techstars because the discipline of hyper-focusing on your business model with the collective help of 50+ really smart people (VCs, CEOs, Founders, etc) is just so helpful. I don't think there are many other places where you can get this kind of authentic, unbiased, un-conflicted application of all these people to figure out what

your business model should be. In a way, Techstars was like having another co-founder in our team.

In fact, accelerator programs feel very similar to the history of the MBA program. The MBA program was a radically different approach at one time to train you for a company. It was considered very niche. If you take the view that the startups going through these accelerators are the "companies of tomorrow," then you might expect accelerators to replace MBAs in some fashion. And to me it's much more of an appropriate education to run a startup than it is to finish an MBA program. Personally, it feels much more fitting to say "I've been through a Techstars accelerator program" than it does for me to say "I did a 2 year MBA program at Stanford." The only thing I regret is that there wasn't some kind of ongoing educational component to the accelerator program once we leave. However, fortunately for us our main investor is Foundry Group and they've taken on that role.

Pre-springboard we were working from different locations, which on occasions could be tricky, so coming together at Google campus was a real help.

Having previously tried to force doors open ourselves, being on the program gave us almost immediate access to the people we wanted to meet and speak to. The mentoring was really valuable, although after week two we did have to lock our CTO away from it all because it can certainly hold up development if you're not careful. That's why having a team of three worked so well for us.

The demo day deadline, although at times frustrating, also brought about a real focus and momentum to what we were doing, and pushed us on to get the product and business in to good shape.

In terms of fundraising it certainly put us in the right circles. You soon learn about how investors view your business. We had been really conscious to build a business that could scale fast and was as lean as possible, so we were able to start having some really good meetings quite early on. *- Dom Lewis – Co-founder, Tray.io (Springboard)*

Being part of Springboard gave me the reassurance I needed to commit to Hassle full time, but it also provided so much more. The mentoring made sure we really understood our business and were able to articulate our value proposition. The networking was insane – it was like a baptism by fire into the startup world, not just in London but across Europe and the US. Springboard also forced us to run quicker than we would normally and pushed us constantly out of our comfort zone. Also, because so much was crammed into twelve weeks, it pushed me to wrap my head around my emotions and check them at the door. Some days I would wake up and think that Hassle was never going to work (usually after a bad mentoring day) and I wanted to throw in the towel. I have learnt that those feelings are a key to success, because they keep you on your toes, constantly questioning if you have it right and how you can improve. *- Alex*

*Depledge – Co-founder, Hassle (Springboard)*

I can't understate the impact Springboard has had on Backscratchers. Obviously it varies depending on the state and size of the company, but for us Springboard did exactly what it said on the tin – took us from A to Z at incredible speed and helped us to build a solid platform from which to launch our business, ensuring we had the best possible chance of survival and success. They challenged and championed us in equal measure, forcing us to regard the business in a different light and from every angle with every possible hat on. We've also met so many clever, influential people through this programme that we would never have had the opportunity to meet otherwise. The support network is fantastic and we've formed lasting relationships with many of the mentors, all of them experts in their field. *- Patrick Elliott – Co-founder, Backscratchers (Springboard)*

Patrick Elliot

All the difference in the world. We went from nobody giving us money to having a menu of investors who wanted to. That was by far the biggest, pleasantly suffocating difference.

The second advantage was the Y Combinator network. Having moved from the East Coast (New York) to the Bay Area, we had no connections. We didn't know anybody. At the end of our Y Combinator batch we became close friends with other founders and, I must say, people tend to underestimate the importance of this. When you're trying not to die, having so many like-minded, supportive friends is extremely comforting and helps you get over the bumps. The extended

YC framework only adds to that. With eleven classes, there will always be an expert to help with whatever you need, from raising money to scaling MongoDB. - *Ev Kontsevoy – Co-founder & CEO, MailGun (Y Combinator)*

RockStart accelerated our company and our entire life. We came to Amsterdam without knowing anybody, with an MVP and a big dream.

It's all about people. The most important thing that the accelerator gives to you is the network. They will give you the opportunity to meet a lot of other founders, entrepreneurs and investors, but then it is up to you to build a relationship with these guys and take the best out of that first meeting. That's your work.

Be ready to disrupt your idea and get out of your comfort zone: sometimes you have to step back to find your focus. Validate your idea being lean and fast in whatever you do, it's all about execution step after step.

We were able to get the focus we were needing, working full time on the project and turn a project into a company. We also managed to get in touch with a lot of entrepreneurs and investors that otherwise would have been very hard to contact. - *Stefano Cutello – Co-founder, PastBook (RockStart)*

Getting into FounderFuel made us realize we could do much more than what we originally wanted to do, and that our potential market is much bigger than what we actually thought.

Access to invaluable mentors. It really is all about the people. There's nothing more valuable than being around people who have built successful businesses who can guide you through the process. They put a light on where you're making mistakes and tell you what they would do if they were you. That kind of hand holding really does accelerate your business; rather than taking three months to figure out something, you'll learn it in one day.

Access to capital. It's hard to start a business on your own. It's easier when you have people ready to give you money so you can focus on the business and have the ability to hire people that can help you grow it. During FounderFuel, we were introduced to many investors, some of them ended up liking our idea and decided they wanted to be part of the adventure.- *Christian Nkurunziza – Co-founder, Tenscores (FounderFund)*

I can't stress enough how important it is to have a community of people doing similar things to you. For at least the first couple of years (if not forever), what you're doing is going to seem pretty crazy to outsiders. Being a part of a group where some really impressive people are also doing seemingly crazy things is an enormous relief from those outside pressures.

Starting a company also leaves you without a lot of mentors. Especially in tech, no one has had the exact set of problems you've had before and often the advice of seasoned experts is dated. With a community, like the one Y Combinator offers, you can still get some of the benefits of a great mentor from the group. When I need to raise money, market more, buy ads, deal with personnel issues, find office space, or any of the other million things that startups need to do as they grow, I can simply grab a drink with a friend or two who've just gone through that specific issue a few months prior and gain a wealth of relevant and up-to-date advice. It's invaluable. - *Dave Fowler – Co-founder & CEO, Chartio (Y Combinator)*

The best experience was certainly the great community of founders in Seedcamp, who all have incredible internal drive. Yet they have saved their humbleness and are super eager to help you out with any challenge, intro or feedback you might ever need. The company benefited from the Seedcamp upbringing – we came out as a much more professional, growth-oriented startup than the couple of idealistic founders who entered. It was tough love. *-Kristo Kaarmann – CEO, TransferWise (Seedcamp)*

It made all the difference in the world, and I would do it again without hesitation. A few of the biggest things that come to mind:

Advice/assistance from the partners: each and every partner added tremendous value for us – from things like helping developing our pitch (both to customers and investors) to introducing us to key customers. It's hard to think of an area of our business that the team didn't help with.

The network: within YC we built lifelong friendships with a number of our batch mates, and I can't count the number of times a YC alumnus has helped us get through a challenge.

Credibility: early customers had more confidence in us because we were part of the program. Additionally, the biggest challenge we're facing now is hiring, and being part of such a great program gives prospective employees a strong vote of confidence in what we're doing. *- Jon Pospischil – Co-founder, Custora (Y Combinator)*

# custora

Y Combinator made a huge difference. A lot of YC alumni say the network and the advice from the partners are the most valuable things. That's undeniably true. Paul Graham has been looking out for us and giving us some really valuable advice, even two and a half years out of the program. He just seems to know the right thing to remind us about. The network is also great. You're basically in a 'founders union', which gives you some power, whereas, typically, power lies with the money (i.e., investors). It's also a fraternity of sorts, and that really helps because the default is failure, so you need all the help you can get. Feeling like you're in this together is great for that, too. That's why you have co-founders, and the rest of YC is sort of like an extended co-founder family. If David had a bunch of friends who were also Davids, then he would've felt more confident about taking on Goliath to execute better and more precisely.

What's the biggest thing for me though? I remember when I first got to Stanford and I felt like I didn't belong because everyone was so amazing. I felt like that again when I got into YC, and everyone was amazing about the thing I'm most passionate about – making a difference in the world through technology by creating great products that people want. Everyone in my batch was an expert at it, and some have already created successful products in the past. That was incredibly motivating. *- Rickey Yean – Co-founder & CEO, Crowdbooster (Y Combinator)*

Dan: I think Y Combinator was a really great opportunity for us to have a focused period of time where all we cared about was building a great product. At the end of Y Combinator you go through demo day, but we knew that those three months were really an opportunity for us to get feedback from Paul Graham, who is undoubtedly the best person to give startup advice in the world. The program was also an opportunity to iterate and be forced to have made progress for every Tuesday night dinner. In fact, it was during Y Combinator that we changed our idea from Spreadly, the product we built before Optimizely, to Optimizely. In the second week, we showed

Paul an early prototype of Optimizely and he was very enthusiastic. He told us it was 'A/B testing for marketers'. At the time I didn't really understand what he meant by that; I was just thinking about the product I would have wanted in 2008 for anyone on my team to do A/B testing. But it turns out marketers are desperate for this solution as well.

Pete: Paul Graham's Rolodex is unbelievable. Given how hard it was to raise money the year before, I was just amazed at how easy he made it. Of course, it was because we put in a ton of work and effort to make an amazing A/B and multivariate testing tool. Having warm introductions to a ton of great investors was super helpful. For us, we'd been trying and failing for almost a year by the time we entered Y Combinator, it was such a shock to our confidence. It felt like we were making progress again for the first time in a while. Psychologically it was a huge boost for us. - *Pete Koomen and Dan Siroker – Co-founders, Optimizely (Y Combinator)*

We had known about Y Combinator for a number of years prior to applying and had always told each other that, if we came up with the right idea, we would apply. As we watched the companies that were coming out of the program, we were really impressed and that sparked an even greater desire to get in. Having gone through the experience, I can say that YC was one of the best things for Gee (co-founder), the company and I. Starting from day one you're thrown into a room with like-minded individuals and teams that are all trying to build something cool. The air just tastes different when you're in that orange room discussing the highs and lows of your week with other people that know exactly where you're coming from. And no, it's not the taste of a hacker that hasn't showered in a week. Imagine Zuckerberg or Pincus talking to you candidly in a small room about how they got started and how they eventually got to where they are now. I don't follow sports much, but a lot

of my friends do and they would give anything for front row tickets to a game or to shake hands with their favorite players. Once a week I got to sit in the front row and shake the hands of my favorite players. I know I sound like I'm drunk off YC Kool-Aid, but it truly was an amazing experience that I'll never forget. - *James Fong – Co-founder, Listia (Y Combinator)*

iAccelerator was a wonderful experience. We were a bunch of tech-strong college students with an idea and an MVP, but in real need of business guidance. The co-working atmosphere was a big, big boon, as we were able to get quick and reliable feedback, and help on hacks we were trying to figure out. With iAccelerator you spend three months on campus at India's best business school. The point is, in India, l33tspeak doesn't always work, so you need to walk the talk with 'guys in suits and boots'. And that's where iAccelerator added value. We got to learn a lot about 'how to write a business plan', marketing strategy and more. The continuous in-house mentorship format always keeps you motivated and maintains a hunger to be ready for the business battle. As a young company approaching the industry, iAccelerator has definitely added a lot more credibility and reliability to the company, which has helped a lot. - *Ankit Gupta – Co-founder, Innovese (iAccelerate)*

There is no way we would be where we are today had it not been for Excelerate Labs and the doors they were able to open for us. Plus, the advice and support didn't stop when the program ended. It's been two years since we graduated Excelerate Labs and we still work closely with our Excelerate advisors and colleagues who went through the program with us. - *Ethan Austin – Founder & CEO, GiveForward (Excelerate Labs)*

# LOCALYTICS

**RAJ AGGARWAL**, Founder
**HENRY CIPOLLA**, Founder
**ANDREW ROLLINS**, Founder

**Founded:** 2008
**Number of Sales:** Used in more than 25,000 apps on over 1.5 billion devices
**Funding raised: $**24.8 Million
**Accelerators:** Techstars Boston (2009)

*Localytics provides a powerful analytics and marketing platform for mobile and web applications. It is used in more than 25,000 apps on more than 1.5 billion devices, helping companies such as ESPN, eBay, Fox, and the New York Times drive user engagement, loyalty, and customer lifetime value.*

I think one of the big things that Techstars did for us was to give some structure and governance. Even in the application process, the motto "Do More Faster" impacted our work ethic. To increase the chance of our application being excepted we were encouraged to give them a weekly update on our progress. We had to be thinking all the time about what we were doing to really push the company forward. Once in the program, we had a weekly check-in with the program's management team and when that was combined with the peer pressure from other companies, it definitely kept us moving faster. The other aspect of the program that really helped was that it brought us deeper into the entrepreneurial tech communities in Boston. We were all first time entrepreneurs so the experience was a bit of a startup boot camp. I had done an MBA before but never a startup, so a lot of these lessons from other entrepreneurs were deeply helpful. Of course we could have gone out and gotten these lessens ourselves but the nice thing about Techstars was that it brought these people to us, as opposed to us needing to go and find them. This really accelerated our ability get started.

During the course of the program, probably the most impactful mentor that we connected with was a guy named called Don McLagan, previously Chairman, President and CEO of Compete which was acquired by Taylor Nelson Sofres, for something like $150m. He really helped us think through the different models that we could follow, using his company and another competing company as two examples of different models. Given that he was the CEO of the company for a number of years, he understood the market intimately. We actually ended up going down a different road from the Compete model. Don's feedback was very helpful in guiding this decision. We had someone familiar with that model telling us all the pitfalls and negatives about things that we might have never thought through or taken a long time to uncover.

To add one final note. During the program my two cofounders and I would fight a lot. It's just how we do things. We yell at each other and we're definitely passionate about what we do. It was a small confined office space so everyone thought we would fall apart and that there was no way we were going to make it as a company. Some of our peers from Techstars are definitely surprised and impressed that 5 years down the road we're still together and have convinced another 97 people to join the team.

# OVERLAY STUDIO, INC

**KEVIN HEAP, Founder**
**SPENCER SMITH, Founder**
**JOE WILSON, Founder**

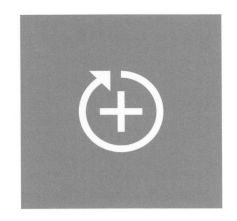

**Founded:** 2013
**Number of Users:** 2.8 Million
**Funding raised:** $1 Million
**Accelerators:** Boom Startup

*Overlay Studio, Inc. develops mobile applications. The company's products include Studio, a design creation and sharing application for iPhone. The company is based in Provo, Utah.*

We've been app developers since day one. We've built over a 144 mobile products for ourselves and other companies. We've even had some relatively well known hits in the App Store. But when we came up with the idea for Studio Design, we knew it was more than just an app. It was a big idea that could offer creative value to millions and millions of people. So we decided to give the idea as much help as possible. Enter Boom Startup.

We had already started building v1 of Studio when we applied to Boom. We had to present a few times, as I think we were in the "iffy" category at first. This is understandable; there are a lot of "photo apps" out there and we were still in the process of articulating how our paradigm was different. Once we were accepted into the program we were very dedicated to participating and absorbing advice. The only thing we weren't on-board with was fundraising.

We had built all our other products with $0 funding. We'd never accepted investment before, and felt we really didn't need to in order to make Studio a success. We were encouraged to be open minded, but ultimately the decision was ours. As Demo Day approached we worked like crazy to get Studio launched. We were able to get the product out 2 weeks before Demo Day. We had great traction by the time we presented – over 240K downloads. Because this metric was so high,

and we were part of an accelerator, investment offers came flooding in. We powwowed as a team, tapped into the advice of our Boom mentors, and made the decision that we could use money to increase our growth rate and build an even better product.

We were able to quickly (2 weeks) close a $1M seed round and get back to work. That was one of the major deciding factors for us. With a team of 4 (our Boom assigned mentor, Brad Hagen, had joined the company by this time) it's hard to spend all your time fundraising. If we aren't building/maintaining the product, no one is. We're still in the middle of that seed round runway, and we've learned a lot of lessons. Most importantly, we learned that having the right investors has been more important than the dollar amount we raised. We have incredible investors here in Utah and in Silicon Valley that have been highly influential in our success so far.

Being part of an accelerator was the reason we were able to get funding and expand our network of advisors/mentors very rapidly. A few people have asked me about raising money. My advice to them is, "you've got to be in the arena." By joining an accelerator, we put ourselves in front of very smart, successful people. Many of these people are still invested in Studio's success.

Y Combinator gave us a crucial piece of advice only a few weeks after we joined their fund. The founding partner, Paul Graham, told us to 'go and be brokers' for a month. He told us to get on a plane, fly back to New York, and just put ourselves in their shoes to make sure that we weren't overlooking anything crucial. He challenged us to discover what part of the job would be the easiest and hardest to replicate on a site.

We went back to New York. We got our real estate licenses and passed the state exams. We ran all around Manhattan photographing apartments while jotting down notes. We gave away six-packs of Coronas to landlords and building superintendents, and they would let us keep keys to their vacant apartments to show potential renters. We met clients daily, including a few pathological types that drive real estate professionals insane. In short, we lived like starving, junior level brokers trying to grind out a living, and we soon realized RentHop was doomed to fail in its current form.

Great real estate brokers add a lot of value and there is no way a computer or website can automate the very human components in a transaction. It was a necessary but demoralizing experience to backtrack on almost all of our early accomplishments. We had an uphill battle to climb to win back the broker community's trust, and our press contacts weren't very happy with our unstable and mixed messaging.

Fortunately, years later we ultimately recovered from the setbacks and, today, thousands of real estate professionals regularly use our service. Brokers contribute more to our revenues than landlords or property managers combined and have become the best source of organic growth! Looking back, that first year was a painful first-hand lesson to avoid premature optimization and to test key assumptions. We were lucky to uncover the flaw early enough thanks to our excellent mentors.

I would absolutely recommend Y Combinator to any startup, even those who have raised angel funding and are quite far along. As a package deal you gain ongoing mentorship, immersion into a three-month intense startup mindset, a network of extremely diverse and successful alumni, and introductions to lots of helpful people. Most importantly, you get a constant morale boost from the regular interactions with other founders in similar situations.- *Lee Lin – Co-founder, RentHop (Y Combinator)*

Above everything, being part of Y Combinator gave us a community of likeminded individuals to hang out with. Doing a startup without a community can be incredibly lonely. With Y Combinator we have a huge community we can reach out to for help.

If you really want to be an entrepreneur, you do not need an accelerator program. Ask yourself a question, would you quit your job for this idea if you didn't get into an incubator? If the answer is no, you are not ready to be an entrepreneur.

Your job as an entrepreneur is to start executing and make accelerators afraid that they're going to miss out on you. There is nothing an investor hates more than missing out on something. Accelerators do not make successful companies: they just pick them first. *- Ben Congleton – Co-founder & CEO, Olark (Y Combinator)*

Flashpoint is an awesome experience. They truly embrace the concept of 'getting out of the building'. In fact, Flashpoint requires this of its participants. You will not learn anything sitting in an office; you have to go out and interact with potential customers. The belief is that this can save a startup from the fate of building a product with no demand, that the founders think addresses a problem, when in reality they are wrong. You want to know whether you are pursuing something that solves a real problem sooner rather than later and that is what Flashpoint does for companies that participate in the program, including ours. Fail fast, before you run out of resources! *- David LaBorde – Co-founder, SwiftPayMD (Flashpoint)*

Although we participated in LaunchBox Digital, we were recently part of the fourth batch of the 500 Startups accelerator program and found it to be significantly more helpful being in Silicon Valley as opposed to being in North Carolina for LBD. While LBD was good in terms of getting my co-founder to quit his full-time job at IBM at the time, plus some initial funding, it frankly didn't have the same vibe, ecosystem and resources that the Bay Area has. LBD gave us the initial validation as first-time entrepreneurs and enabled us to be more confident about what we could achieve, and how we could impact the world with our product and technology. One and a half years later, 500 Startups is tremendously helpful in injecting us into the heart of Silicon Valley (CityPockets/Reclip. It was based in NYC before that) and connecting us with so many amazing mentors and advisors that have so much knowledge in design, product and distribution. There's just something about the vibe and energy in the valley that births so many incredible startups that are on the bleeding edge of technology. And it's so inspiring to be part of this community that I think makes a difference when you're starting out as an entrepreneur. - *Cheryl Yeoh – Co-founder & CEO, Reclip.It (LaunchBox Digital and 500 Startups)*

Being part of Startmate has been the most memorable and rewarding experience in our business so far. We had the privilege of working closely with twenty-five mentors, and then flown to the US for a capital raising tour. The wealth of knowledge gained from the experience was not only invaluable, but also tremendously helped to refine our business. In those three months in the program, we learned far more than we would have in three years. - *Marianne Sea – Co-founder, Young Republic (StartMate)*

H-Farm is that wise guide. We are learning a lot of things and the power of this acceleration program is not in their investment in terms of money, but in the quality of people that we connect with. Humanity, experience and collaboration are the key for our growth in this program and we absolutely like this approach. - *Vincenzo Acinapura – Co-founder & Technical Director, Foooblr (H-Farm)*

We were out of money and literally going to shut the company down if we didn't get into Techstars, so for us it made all the difference in the world! But seriously, if you are a first-time entrepreneur in the 'wild', there are two problems.

The first is that each coffee, lunch or random meeting seems to carry equal weight, meaning that it is hard to discern who will genuinely add value to your business versus those who are trying to take advantage of entrepreneurs or string you along with talk of investing, but will never actually cut a cheque.

The second issue is that, when you are trying to raise your first capital as a new entrepreneur, there is very little incentive for any investor to act. Each day that goes by, you and your team grow more desperate for the cash (so they can get better terms) and they learn more about your business as you build product, sell and recruit.

Techstars solves both of these problems by creating a safe, pre-screened mentor network (leeches were weeded out long ago) and demo day creates artificial time pressure and scarcity which motivates investors to actually put down term sheets and invest their capital. - *Alex White – Co-founder & CEO, NextBigSound (Techstars)*

'Without Techstars, I'm not sure we would have a company.'

Techstars provided the funding to get started, the focus to learn and build a tremendous amount in a short period of time, and the network of mentors, partners and customers needed to make an idea into a business. Without Techstars, I'm not sure we would have a company.

This can't be overstated: the true value of an accelerator is the network. Once you become a node on the network, it is up to you to effectively traverse it and find the meaningful introductions that can change the course of your business. The network lasts far after the accelerator program is over, and continues to provide value if you actively engage it. *- Justin DeLay – Co-founder, TempoDB (Techstars)*

Techstars, especially our class – the first in NYC – was one of the most insanely productive periods of our life as a startup. When you literally have a timer on all the monitors counting down the days, hours, minutes and seconds until demo day … the pressure is intense, so you have to perform.

But to counteract that, you're going through it with ten other companies and you all help each other through it. I'm still close with everyone and it's great that we all help and support one another. That's just within my class, but the larger network of Techstars is just as powerful. It's awesome to show up to a Techstars city and know you've got a friend *- Reece Pacheco – Founder & CEO, Shelby.tv (Techstars)*

Getting early introductions to managers through the Techstars mentor network let us know immediately that we didn't understand our customer. The product we were building was great for individual employees, but horrible for managers. This led us to close our laptops for the first month of the three-month program, and we simply spent all of that time meeting with users and learning everything we could about their needs. This was an extremely tough thing for us to do. As software engineers, our natural state is to be programming. When we don't know what else to do with ourselves, we gravitate towards our keyboards.

Techstars put us in a position where we quickly learned that we had no idea who our real customer was, and the program enabled us to spend a whole month learning about what we should be building. It would have been near impossible to get the quality and quantity of introductions that we were getting without Techstars.

Having mentors, who have had their own successes, giving us guidance on how to build a company was also invaluable. We wound up bringing on two of our Techstars mentors as formal advisors after the program finished.

They say that luck is the intersection between opportunity and preparedness. Techstars provides both opportunities and preparation. It's like a luck multiplier. You can make your own luck, and you'll certainly have to in order to succeed, but Techstars gives a huge initial boost to first-time founders. *- Steve Krenzel and Brandon Bloom – Co-founders, Thinkfuse (Techstars)*

1. The quality of the mentor network was simply incredible. For anything we were struggling with, there'd be someone with deep experience who had faced the same problem before. We also met a number of the people who ultimately became ongoing advisors and investors through the program.

2. We went through the program with an incredible cohort of fellow entrepreneurs, mostly at the same stage of development as we were. The camaraderie and encouragement really help with the rough moments, and make the whole journey a little less lonely. That's continued post-program.

3. Finally, the sheer number of reactions you get from people involved with the program is incredibly helpful in refining your vision and forces you to test it against reality. *- Todd Silverstein – Co-founder & CEO, Vizify (Techstars)*

Joining the 500 Startups team was crucial to VidCaster's evolution in becoming the company it is today. VidCaster joined 500 Startups in 2011 as part of their second batch of companies to participate in their accelerator program in Mountain View. Before joining 500 we had been fundraising for a traditional seed round, so when we heard that 500 was interested we were a bit hesitant at the concept of joining an incubator. But, after spending the summer with the 500 crew and other portfolio companies in their Mountain View office, we soon changed our tune.

The most valuable aspect of the 500 Startups program was orientating our team to build a true company around our already strong foundation of technology and core product. Our team is composed of great technologists with deep experience with online video infrastructure, but we had gaps in our sales and marketing experience. Through the 500 Startups program benefits, including expert mentoring, on-site seminars and frequent one-on-one time with their experienced staff, we were able to build the proper sales and marketing infrastructure around the VidCaster product, which has led to quick adoption across the tech company sector to drive measurable video marketing. *- Kieran Farr – Co-founder & CEO, VidCaster (500 Startups)*

500 Startups made a lot of sense for us because it was clear the value they would bring was more than just financial. I'm a believer that there isn't nearly as much sharing of best practices among startups as there could be, or should be. That's one of the key ways that 500 Startups has been a tremendous resource for us. It's a vibrant community of startups that are consistently looking for opportunities to share best practices, provide key introductions, and generally support one another.

With hundreds of bright and talented entrepreneurs in the portfolio, it's also a great place to seek out advice on a variety of topics, from some critical strategic questions all the way down to mundane administrative issues. 500 Startups brings even more depth to this by lining up literally hundreds of mentors who are willing to pitch in on their areas of expertise to help propel forward portfolio companies. Similarly, even though there are now literally hundreds of companies in the portfolio, Dave McClure and his team still do a great job at making themselves available to help. *- Karl Sun – Co-founder & CEO, and Ben Dilts – Co-founder & CTO, Lucidchart (500 Startups)*

Starting a company is probably the hardest thing you can do in life, but 500 Startups makes it a lot easier. We didn't know anyone when we moved to Silicon Valley, but 500 Startups opened an unbelievable network of investors and mentors that have been key to our success so far. It's impossible to overstate how valuable it is to sit down for one-on-one meetings with the president of PayPal, or the founder of BillMeLater, but this is the type of access 500 facilitates. *- Camilo Acosta – Co-founder & CEO, PayByGroup (500 Startups)*

The accelerator really helps in getting rid of a lot of myths about building a company, and reveals a lot of the science about building a company. 500 Startups has a very strong focus on three key disciplines:

Design: strong focus on target audience and keeping that in mind when designing your product.
Data: measure almost everything e.g.,basic metrics, but also measure the impact when launching new features.
Distribution: identify the best channels to get your product to the market. *- Khuram Hussain – Co-founder & CEO, Fileboard (500 Startups)*

*'It was like entrepreneur grad school on crack.'*

# UBOOLY

**CARLY GLOGE, Founder**
**ISAAC SQUIRES, Founder**
**GAVIN LEE, Founder**

**Founded:** 2012
**Units Sold:** 40,000
**Funding raised:** $2.5 Million
**Accelerators:** Techstars Boulder (2012)

*Ubooly is a stuffed animal for children that talks and listens. Ubooly can be customized to know a child's name, teach lessons, and much more. The company was started in much the same way as Accelerate, through a Kickstarter project. At the completion of their project, Ubooly had raised more than $50,000, double their goal. As an interesting side note, their acceptance into the Techstars program was partly contingent on the success of the Kickstarter campaign, which was run alongside their application process to the program.*

Possibly one of the biggest learning experiences for us during Techstars was how to market the product to consumers, but also how to describe what we're doing in a way that's compelling to VCs. Convincing VCs to give us enough money to build a stuffed animal was a tricky venture on its own, and Techstars definitely made this an easier landscape to traverse than it would have otherwise been.

One of the most incredibly helpful things to us during the program was to meet with true tested CEOs. We sat down and shared experiences through which they could help us navigate. During the program we had our first acquisition offer, which we ultimately declined. While going through the offer it was so valuable to be able to sit down with CEOs that had experienced acquisitions, where we could candidly discuss their first acquisition and how they handled it. If you think about it, the internet is a really wonderful thing where you can ask all sorts of anonymous questions and get all sorts of anonymous answers back, but having a real one-on-one with others that have been there and done it, in an off-the-record format that allowed them to talk about details that they otherwise may not be able to discuss, was incredible.

The accelerator experience isn't all smooth sailing – there's a learning curve and it's a steep one. One thing that we had to deal with was Demo Day and our first product shipment deadline was happening at the same time. When we initially prototyped the product we used silicone foam which was way too expensive to manufacture, so the plan was to switch to something called CPR gel. It seemed like it was going to work, we received some initial samples that looked great. It was getting close to Demo Day and, for some crazy reason, we felt that it was important to ship the product alongside the big event. So, instead of getting a final production sample, we decided we would just look at the product in China over webcam and make the call. Great choice! We saw this toy on webcam and it looked beautiful, but when it arrived in Colorado it looked like it had eaten six chocolate bars on the trip over. What we found was that there were pockets of air in the gel so at high altitude our toys were exploding.

We actually shipped some units directly from the factory to our Kickstarter supporters. Some of the toys became so fat that their seams exploded — hilarious in hindsight but shocking and nerve-wracking in the moment. Everything turned out fine — it was non-toxic gel and we replaced the units, but this was definitely something we didn't expect we'd experience when entering the program.

500 Startups was an invaluable experience for us. It was like entrepreneur grad school on crack. We went from being UI/UX design and data noobs, to obsessing over these things, seeking out newer and better tools to improve our process, and growing our network of fellow entrepreneurs and mentors who could help us succeed. One of the most amazing things about 500 is how large and powerful the network is. You can get deep insights into nearly any problem you are facing by asking a question to the 500 community, or reaching out to others in the community.

Dave McClure must have been a bit crazy. At the time we were based in Seattle, and in Seattle we had gotten really focused on traction and growing our number of paying customers, so all this helped. Dave knew a lot about our market having been involved in SimplyHired, so I think he recognized better than nearly any other investor how big a market college recruiting really is. We also owe an infinite amount of thanks to Dave Schappell, who has been a phenomenal advisor to our company and helped introduce us to Dave McClure while we were still in Seattle. *- Nathan Parcells – Co-founder & CMO, InternMatch (500 Startups)*

Techstars has been an incredible experience for our company. We were all living in Miami before the program, and weren't plugged into business and technology communities. Within the first week of the program we made more contacts than we would have made in a year in Miami. We also had a great support system in the program. Twelve other companies were going through Techstars with us, and everyone was great about helping each other out. We also can't say enough good things about David Tisch and Adam Rothenberg. They have been by far our biggest supporters. *- Katrina Brickner – Co-founder, Marquee (Techstars)*

In addition to the experience itself, the network that we gained by being part of this was an enormous help. As I mentioned above, fundraising in Boise is challenging, but the relationships we built through Techstars of mentors, investors and colleagues has made a huge difference. *- Wink Jones – Co-founder & CEO, Mealticket (Techstars)*

For us, it was transformative. I'm not sure that we would have gotten here without having gone through AngelPad. The program forced us to drop our pencils, step back and re-evaluate everything. It didn't matter if it was working or not. Of course, the other advantage of a program like AngelPad is the network access. The program has opened the door to not only investors, but an incredible group of founders/companies that support one another. *- Dana Severson – Co-founder & CEO, Chasm.io (AngelPad)*

For us, the Techstars program was life changing. Of course, not every accelerator is the same. As teachers and learners, we really appreciated Techstars' focus on mentorship. The chance to engage really deeply with a few people allowed us to safely re-examine the direction in which we were headed. We took much more of a consumer turn during the program. It also dramatically expanded the circle of people we can call when we have questions, and, of course, the structure of Demo Day at the end of the program helped us raise funding more quickly and easily than we would have been able to do on our own. *- Miro Kazakoff - Co-founder & CEO, and Tom Rose – Co-founder & CPO, Testive (Techstars)*

Everything at TS is driven by what the customer wants, so we do a lot of customer development and that becomes engrained in the company *- Manuel Medina – Co-founder & CEO, Grouptalent*

# LET GUST HELP YOU NAVIGATE THE FUNDRAISING MAZE

Gust is the leading fundraising platform for startups worldwide. With more than $1.8 billion invested through our platform, Gust makes it easy to venture forward. Get on board. Get funded. Sign up for free at **gust.com**

# DIGITALOCEAN

**BEN URETSKY,** Founder
**JEFF CARR,** Founder
**MOISEY URETSKY,** Founder
**MITCH WAINER,** Founder
**ALEC HARTMAN,** Founder

**Founded:** 2011
**Subscribers:** 258,571
**Funding raised:** $40.2 Million
**Accelerators:** Techstars Boulder (2012)

*DigitalOcean is passionate about making complex infrastructure simple for their users with a seamless enjoyable experience. DigitalOcean is a cloud hosting service built for developers. Customers can create a cloud server in under a minute, with servers located in New York, San Francisco, and Amsterdam.*

During our accelerator experience, we had a handful of amazing mentors that helped shape our product and focus our vision for DigitalOcean. However, it was Jason Seats who had the most significant impact, contributing some of the key ideas that helped us understand the market and drive DigitalOcean's growth. For example, one of the things Jason was adamant about was not paying for marketing. He felt building organic awareness, and acquiring customers through strong content, was a very important part of the business.

It was also Jason's idea to promote the community around our service, so we poured a lot of resources into curating a library of tutorials on open source and sysadmin topics. Today we have over a thousand articles, with hundreds of thousands of users participating in the discussions around those articles, whether it's through submitting one of their own for publication to answering questions in the community. And what's great is that all of these tutorials bring in a ton of customers – we are getting nearly two million unique visits to the community section of our website every month.

This is all part of our marketing strategy, and it allows us to cut the cost of customer acquisitions in half because of how efficient it is at delivering the right people to our site. We can target our ads and build brand credibility based on the information that we are discussing. Ultimately, DigitalOcean is introduced to millions of people around the world at a much faster and affordable rate than pay per click advertising. And it's thanks to Jason's strong belief in organic marketing and building community that DigitalOcean was able to scale so quickly. But we also believed that paying to acquire the right customers, when done strategically, could be an effective method of driving growth. So Mitch, our CMO, used an ideal combination of both of these elements to help bring DigitalOcean to where it is today.

Jason's advice would challenge our beliefs, but it was always with the intent of building a more successful company. If we look at the bigger picture, with over 100 mentors in the program, we certainly felt a lot mentor whiplash – and not everyone was always on the same page. Some would tell us that we needed to target more for our product, while others questioned our ability to compete with Amazon. A few even suggested pivoting to something completely different, because they didn't see how we could make a dent in the market. But each time we'd attempt to do something else, we found ourselves returning to our original hypothesis around simplifying cloud infrastructure. At the end of the day, it was good to be challenged and forced to see things from different perspectives, but our passion for empowering developers would lead us to devoting 100% of our energy behind the original concept for DigitalOcean.

When it came to our demo day experience, there was certainly pressure to raise capital in conjunction with the presentation. I feel as though that may not always be the best course of action – it's easy to over-focus on it and lose sight of other important aspects of maturing your company. We tried to raise a $500,000 seed round exiting demo day and it took us about two and a half months to claw enough investors together. It was a very difficult process; we had about 12 or 13 different participants that would sign up then drop out.

When we took some time to step back and look at the business, we realized we were growing faster than we initially anticipated, and we weren't even confident that $500,000 would provide sufficient runway in exchange for the equity that we were giving out. After reflecting on the bigger picture, we made the right decision and chose to cancel the seed round. We were able to continue operating for another six months until we engaged with IA Ventures, who then restarted the round where we raised $3.2 million in the summer of 2013. We have since gone on to raise an additional $37 million, led by venture capital firm a16z.

# PROBLEMS

# LESSONS

# FACED &
# LEARNED

# PROBLEMS FACED & LESSONS LEARNED

The journey through an accelerator is more often about failing quickly than succeeding slowly. Much of the structure of an accelerator is in place to reveal flaws in the business and product as quickly as possible, then to solve those flaws as quickly as possible. Take the high-intensity mentor meetings as an example. The goal is to get as many eyes and brain cells on the business so if there are any gaps in the core business, hopefully they will come to the surface. Many accelerators also preach Lean Startup or other methodologies that are costumer development and product validation centric. This is towards the same end of throwing the business model and product against customers to see where the breaking points are.

The entire experience of an accelerator is a test for the team. The long hours, the competitive pressure from other teams, and the countdown to Demo Day are all highly stressful aspects of every program. Undoubtedly, there are people and teams that break under this stress. This is the goal to some degree. If a team cannot persevere through an accelerator, they are most likely in no position to run a startup and deal with the even more stressful circumstances down the road. Going back to the "fast fail" mentality of accelerators, teams either fall apart during the program or they come out forged by fire and stronger because of it.

With that in mind, there are a lot of problems faced whens starting a company and, hopefully, a lot of lessons learned through the course of an accelerator. In this section, founders discuss their startup problems frankly and openly, and even address problems that were large enough to put the company in the graveyard.

500

The hardest part about starting a business has been getting access to the right people and making sure there's a few quid in the bank. We managed to sell cars, use credit cards, basically beg and borrow to give us the chance to be able to work away on our business. It can be really tough having to turn down going out and meeting friends, but with enough belief in what you're doing and a pretty clear idea of where you want to go, it's worth it. Plus there's a lot you can do with pasta.

The other big challenge is getting access to the right people. Although partly down to location, we found finding people who could give us the right advice and open the right doors was very difficult, because good people are always very busy and you're never their number one priority. I can't stress the importance of networking highly enough. Meet as many people as you can and build good circles around your business. They might not seem useful at the time, but the right people can massively help make your business. Our experience at the accelerator Springboard was huge for us in that respect. *- Dom Lewis – Co-founder, Tray.io (Springboard)*

## 'Keeping a roof over your head and food in your mouth has to be a priority.'

There were so many ... but the two biggest ones would be deciding whether or not it needed to be a tech company and understanding that it is okay to charge for our service.

My background is not a technical one, but to be able to provide the service that I wanted relied on us being a technology company. So I decided to teach myself how to program. Being able to code myself also made it easier to find other developers willing to join the band, while giving me a deeper understanding of the process needed to bring by idea from concept to reality.

The second biggest challenge was to convince

myself that the product is worth paying for and then asking customers to pay for it. This might sound easy, but asking people to pay can be quite a daunting task when you startup. Even now, I still find myself almost apologizing for charging. But our customers are happy paying and that makes us happy. *- David Buxton – Founder, Arachnys (Springboard)*

One of the very first challenges we faced was finding the right people to help us build the platform. Lots of people saw the value in a product like ours, but convincing them to follow our lead and make the idea a reality was often tough. Some people really don't like uncertainty and are averse to taking risks (especially financial ones). After months of searching, we found the perfect person, Leo Critchley. Leo is now our CTO, an accomplished developer but also a published author and illustrator. He understood both sides of the business and, once he knew what we were trying to do, he jumped on board.

Another challenge was the lack of resources (money!) and time to focus on the business. Keeping a roof over your head and food in your mouth has to be a priority, so for a while we were working all sorts of crazy hours outside our other full-time jobs – standard startup initiation. Finally, there's the mandatory forgoing of friends, frivolity, and weekends. *- Patrick Elliott – Co-founder, Backscratchers (Springboard)*

We all had good jobs, financial commitments and leaving that behind is hard (at first), but then Springboard was the external validation we needed to propel us out of the door and realize our idea wasn't simply daft.

Skills. None of the team are developers by trade. We thought at first (like true consultants) we would write a business plan and hire developers, but we soon realized that it was a) daft and b) too risky, as we needed to own and understand our technology. So Jules and Tom (Thomas Nimmo, fellow co-founder) started in PHP and were soon advised to switch to Ruby, so we bought a book and have never looked back. *- Alex Depledge – Co-founder, Hassle (Springboard)*

Alex Depledge

Nobody would give us money. Potential employees and co-founders would refuse to join us. Landlords in San Francisco would not accept my application. The fundamental fact is that, when you are starting a company, you are in the business of not dying. Being a cockroach in the middle of a highway and staying alive was the biggest challenge.

There were marketing issues as well. Selling APIs did not sound like a hot business plan in 2009. APIs were usually seen as a free add-on to a revenue-generating product, not as a product by themselves. Amazon Web Services and Twilio helped changed that. *- Ev Kontsevoy – Co-founder & CEO, MailGun (Y Combinator)*

I went from being a consultant, to having the service business, to pivoting into a product company. I did it gradually, but each step came with its own challenges. The biggest one is learning to manage people and getting everyone to do their best, even when the going gets tough. There is only so much you can read about or talk to peers about, the rest is cold, hard learning while doing. Mistakes will be made, but learning from this is crucial. Understanding what you are good at and not good at was another. At first you feel you have to be good at everything and know everything. Learning to back down and focus on the elements you can do and do well is crucial. It is difficult learning and admitting when you are not good at something, then having the patience and trust for someone else to do it. But once you learn to give territory, things can become smoother. *- Jude Ower – Founder, PlayMob (Springboard)*

> 'If I hadn't met my co-founder, Tenscores probably wouldn't be here.'

Being able to keep going even in the face of failure. Before Tenscores, I tried a lot of things that didn't work. I learned a lot from them. Someone said, 'Sometimes you win, sometimes you learn.' That is true.

Finding great people that can help is crucial as well, and very hard to do. If I hadn't met my co-founder, Tenscores probably wouldn't be here. If we hadn't met with the guys from FounderFuel, we wouldn't be where we are. If we hadn't found the great programmers we hired recently, we wouldn't be planning our next launch right now. So there is a series of events driven by people that contribute to the success of a business. Finding those people is no easy task. *- Christian Nkurunziza – Co-founder, Tenscores (FounderFuel)*

I always think that one of the hardest, and least expected, difficulties of starting a company is just making people realize that you exist. People write about virality, advertising, etc., but it always slides over the first stages when you're three founders sitting in a room with a great idea, trying to get people to simply know about you. It's a constant struggle, and it drives your strategy at every point. *- Aaron Harris – Co-founder & CEO, Tutorspree (Y Combinator)*

Staying focused on the right things – there are far more directions you can pursue than there is time to pursue them. For example, we started out with two products, one for subscription businesses and another for retail-style businesses. It took us a while to zoom in and focus just on the retail-style companies – we had to turn away revenue and some high-profile clients, and that was really hard to do when we were just getting going. We feel the benefits now as our product is more tailored for retail marketing needs and, therefore, much more valuable. But it was a hard decision to make, and one that we certainly made later than we should have.*- Jon Pospischil – Co-founder, Custora (Y Combinator)*

I had two primary challenges. One: I was a single founder, so everything initially depended solely on me. It was good in the sense that I could make decisions and act quickly, but it was also very lonely at times. Two: I embarked on building a complex product that needed to be relatively mature before I could start to see real adoption. After two years, we've finally hit that point, but it has been a long road in getting here. This does provide us with some defensibility, but I've often found myself looking longingly at other products that just did one simple thing very well. *- Ray Grieselhuber – Co-founder & CEO, GinzaMetrics (Y Combinator)*

# ıllı GinzaMetrics

I would say that our main challenge was settling on a product to work on. When we got together, we were both interested in behaviour change space e.g., apps that help you form habits. We

tried a few ideas in this space, but we were scatterbrained, and I think we switched between ideas too rapidly. Some of our ideas were also not that good.

Once we started working on WorkFlowy, things have actually gone relatively smoothly. ('Relatively' is an important word here, because things never go that smoothly in startup-land.) We launched the product publicly in November 2010 and we got great reactions immediately. We had 20,000 signups within a couple of weeks and all sorts of praise for the product was flowing in. This was awesome for us, because the product was still quite rudimentary and we knew there was still a ton to do to improve it.

We did take longer than either of us would have liked to roll out our premium offering – WorkFlowy Pro. We launched that in March 2013, and it's been doing quite well so far. The percentage of our users who've upgrade to Pro is comparable to other freemium services like Evernote and Dropbox.

I do think that we waited too long to release the Pro version, though. This was because we really like to work on features that improve the product immediately, and we also were worried that we'd get it wrong and wanted to be sure that it would work out.

*- Mike Turitzin – Co-founder, WorkFlowy (Y Combinator)*

Financial services innovation is really hard. There are many notable hurdles, including, but not limited to, security, privacy, and regulatory concerns. In our case, one of the earliest challenges was having enough capital in order to securely integrate financial data into the product. As a startup, it was cost-prohibitive and difficult to work with integrations that were designed for much larger financial institutions. *- Rod Ebrahimi – Co-founder & CEO, ReadyForZero (Y Combinator)*

Dan: The first company we started was CarrotSticks, an online math game for kids. One of the bigger challenges we faced with this company was not knowing the core audience we were building for since we weren't parents, teachers, or kids. I think that was a root cause of a lot of the problems we had along the way. Comparing that experience to what we're doing now with Optimizely, we're building the product I wish we had had in 2008. So the early decisions around what's important and what's not have been much easier with Optimizely than with CarrotSticks.

Pete: During that experience we also learned how valuable it was to really listen to your customers or your potential customers. With CarrotSticks, it took us eight months to earn our first dollar. With Optimizely, it took us one day. The key, we learned, was to stop trusting our own instincts and start listening to our customers. *- Pete Koomen and Dan Siroker – Co-founders, Optimizely (Y Combinator)*

We had the classic chicken and egg problem trying to start a marketplace from scratch. Because we use a virtual currency, we decided to give every new user credits when they signed up and this essentially made every user on our site a buyer. We assumed we had buyers, but how would we get sellers? Clean out everything in our homes of course! We gathered all the stuff from our homes, put it in a pile and had it all ready to go when we launched the site. We also made routine trips to Fry's and bought hundreds of $1 to $5 items to list as well. We have this concept of Rewards Auctions where Listia will sell brand new items to reward our most active users and when we launched we listed a LCD TV and some headphones. To top it off, we knew we would get a large influx of tech-savvy Silicon Valley hackers at launch, so we begged Paul Graham to let us raid his house. What hacker wouldn't want an out of print copy of *On Lisp* signed by Paul Graham? It turned out a lot of people wanted Paul Graham anything. Our guess was that if every new user started with the same number of credits, a few

would try to get an edge on the competition by listing their own stuff for more credits. I think it worked pretty well. *- James Fong – Co-founder, Listia (Y Combinator)*

## 'Nothing prepares you for founding a startup besides founding a startup.'

Here are some of our challenges and what I'd do differently if I had a time machine:

Spend a lot more time on user acquisition: I've found distribution and user acquisition just as challenging as building a great product. Raising awareness of our product, building a community of fans, growing active email lists, and Twitter followers are just as important as five-star reviews on iTunes. Also, engaging press early, getting to know influential writers, bloggers, etc. It's much easier to build genuine relationships with people when you don't have to ask them for anything. It's a little late to try to get to know journalists or writers the night before your launch. So learning how to build these resources early on for your company is quite important.

Start building a network of advisors and potential investors a lot earlier: from talking to many people in the valley, I think finding advisors and investors is really a matter of meeting other like-minded people with resources who want to help you out. It's much easier to get help when they naturally buy into your crazy idea without your having to convince them in the first place. Despite all the advances in networking tools which we have today – Twitter, Linkedin, Angelist, etc., there's still a fairly large element of serendipity and human networking involved, all of which takes a lot of time.

Do the startup a lot earlier: nothing prepares you for founding a startup besides founding a startup.

Being an early employee helps, but it's still not the same. So just jump in. *- Yu-Kuan Lin, Co-founder, Everyday.me (Y Combinator)*

To be perfectly honest, I'd say we're still at the 'very beginning,' even after having been around almost two years! That said, the biggest challenges we've faced are:

1. Shipping. Soon after deciding to start Tumult and build Hype, we heard of other companies working on similar tools. Knowing a major company's entering our product space created a unique sense of urgency, but it was critical we struck the right balance between our feature set and our ship date. If we shipped with too few or the wrong features, we'd waste our launch buzz and possibly burn customer goodwill; but if we kept adding features and waited too long to ship, someone else might capture the market before we could make a splash. Unfortunately, I can't offer any universal advice for others facing this same challenge. Striking that balance requires an understanding of your potential customers and having some intuition where your competitors stand. People preach about minimum viable products, but finding that local maximum of 'minimum viability' is incredibly tricky. That said, at some point you must ship. Real artists ship.

2. Awareness. Unless you're lucky enough to get tons of free press or you're already famous, no one knows about your company. You may be building the best app, site or service ever made, but it doesn't matter one bit if no one actually sees it. The only answer to this challenge is hustle. Reach out to anyone who will listen, stay on message, and evangelize every chance you get. Consider spending some of your precious cash reserves on advertising. Tweet, post, blog, and network like crazy. Try everything you can, but always have a way to evaluate the efficacy of each experiment. If you don't have a way of evaluating results, you won't know where to focus your limited resources.

In our case, we attracted the attention of some rather influential bloggers and tweeters, which drove an incredible amount of initial traffic and sales. The App Store gods have also smiled upon us and featured Hype a number of times. Almost all of our awareness thus far has come from leveraging our network and choosing to ride the HTML5 tidal wave when we did.

3. Growing. You've built an awesome product, people know about it and revenue is rolling in? Fantastic! Now you need to turn those hundreds into thousands, and those thousands into millions. You need to build a strong, cohesive team with a culture you're proud of. Your customers need to be supported, and ideally fostered into a community that amplifies your product.

All while doing this, you'll face not just execution challenges, but existential challenges – do you want to raise money or bootstrap? Do you want to build a team as quickly as possible or instead grow slowly and organically, carefully picking each new hire? Should you build a sales team or hire more engineers, and what about some designers? There are no right or wrong answers, but these are just a few of the questions that must be answered before you can grow effectively and appropriately for your long-term goals.

I can't say we've overcome the growth challenge … no company that's still alive ever does! *- Ryan Nielsen – Co-founder, Tumult (Y Combinator)*

There were too many to count! Anyone who tells you a startup story that isn't fraught with 'WIFO' moments (We're-Screwed-It's-Over) isn't telling the truth; there are always a ton of challenges. The challenges we faced (in no particular order) are: being so broke I could barely sleep at night; having extremely well-funded competition; hearing 98 of the first 100 investors we pitched to tell me our idea was bad. Sometimes, you have to get out of the startup bubble. Reading TechCrunch or going to tech events, you feel like everyone's getting funded by Andreessen and all other companies are 'going GREAT!' Guess what – in this industry, people will tell you that right up until they have to shut down because they have no customers. Ignore the hype machine. Everyone has challenges – everyone. You just have to focus on beating yours. *- Kathryn Minshew, – Co-founder & CEO, The Daily Muse (Y Combinator)*

Starting a company is incredibly hard. Building a founding team is incredibly hard. Firing people is incredibly hard. Bootstrapping to profitability is incredibly hard. Starting a company is one challenge after another. If you don't love solving problems, you're not going to like being an entrepreneur.

The founding team of Olark changed at least four times before we found the right set of co-founders to build this company. *- Ben Congleton – Co-founder & CEO, Olark (Y Combinator)*

The single most important thing and greatest challenge as an entrepreneur is finding the right people to join you in your quest for revolution. It can be hard finding people that want to commit their lives to making a startup succeed. And when you do find them, make sure they have the right balance of direction and freedom to truly set the world on fire. *- Seth Priebatsch – Chief Ninja, LevelUp (DreamIt)*

Building the right team was quite a challenge. Everybody loves the idea of working on a startup, but just a few people have the guts, the ability ,and the focus to pull it through. Finding them is one of the hardest tasks and, although we're still a young company, we already have our share of bad experiences in this direction. We hope we've learned from them. *- Oliver Lukesch – Co-founder & CEO, Weavly (SUBC)*

With any new technology platform which tries to change an existing online culture, the biggest hurdle is to settle it well among the stakeholders (publishers/advertisers) mandate. By that I mean, make them understand the true potential and the reliability of the platform. *- Ankit Gupta – Co-founder, Innovese (iAccelerate)*

We are five guys who started doing colored.by as a side project, so we had to coordinate our working hours and often work remotely. We also wanted colored.by to be internationally orientated, so deciding on language, legal forms, and regions to concentrate on first was a tough decission. *- Christian Atz – Co-founder, colored.by (iAccelerate)*

'If you don't love solving problems, you're not going to like being an entrepreneur.'

If you are a non-technical founder, it's always hard launching ambitious technical products unless you have an engineering team that you have worked with before, which I didn't because my prior startup eCrush wasn't based in LA and I had non-solicitation agreements as part of the exit. So it took a lot longer than planned to launch and to get a core technical team that really jelled. There were thousands of other challenges as well, but since this is my fifth startup, none of them were completely unexpected, though you tend to forget how time-consuming they can be. Starting anything ambitious is all-consuming. *- Clark Benson – Founder & CEO, Ranker (LaunchPad LA)*

Where do we start? We had zero budget, no staff, and a service that the public didn't quite yet understand. Initially, we were trying to be all things to all people (fundraising for anything), which made it difficult to gain traction with any one demographic. But once we listened to our users – who were mainly using the site to raise money for medical expenses – and we pivoted to focus on fundraising for out-of-pocket medical expenses, we saw tremendous success. You'll hear it time and time again, but don't be afraid to listen to what your users are telling you. *- Ethan Austin – Founder & CEO, GiveForward (Excelerate Labs)*

The biggest challenge in any startup is truly validating what you propose doing before you build anything. Building something is so easy and often (incorrectly) seems like the most important and logical thing to do out of the starting blocks. Too many failed startups spend a lot of capital and time building a solution before they have truly determined it addresses a pain point that is large enough, that people truly need, and one for which there are a large number of customers that will PAY. The highest and best use of any startup founder's time is validation of the concept, which will substantially reduce the risk of the venture.

*- David LaBorde – Co-founder, SwiftPayMD (Flashpoint)*

A key challenge we faced was our desire to jump straight into the traditional product development process. We were, and still are, extremely confident in the opportunity to provide SMBs the same ecommerce marketing tools that big businesses like Amazon exploit. The opportunity is so big that we wanted to dive right in. We resisted this temptation and elected to follow the lean launch startup model. We've been following the customer discovery process and it has yielded significant returns. We're even more convinced of the magnitude of the opportunity and, most importantly, we've gained valuable insights into the needs and desires of the small ecommerce merchant. *- Joe Reger Jr. – Co-founder, Springbot (Flashpoint)*

The background of both of us co-founders was not very 'suitable' for this task. Mikko is an electrical engineer and I worked as a laser scientist, though we both met when studying Industrial Management. Neither of us was a coder, gamer, guitar player, or teacher, or had any experience in audio technology or any adjacent field in which Ovelin operates. The only real 'insight' we brought to the table was our experience as guitar dropouts. However, maybe because of this outside view we were able to keep the focus on what matters and, in the meantime, hired the best game developers, audio scientist, music teachers, and visual artists out there to build the product.

Obviously, it was not very easy for us to raise money, but we managed to get a first prototype built, were able to build excitement and launch the product with FFF and some governmental support money. After it became clear that WildChords was popular, fundraising was easier. *- Chris Thür – Co-founder & CEO, Ovelin (Startup Sauna)*

Marci (Co-founder) and I knew the problems we wanted to solve, and, of course, that is important when you're going to start a company. We had lived and breathed them, and spent months thinking about viable solutions — but actually starting the company was a different experience. We learned as we went along.

One of the biggest challenges for a startup like ours is not unique: how do we bring in money? We've relied on the help of friends and our families, and angel investments, and we continue to look for additional investments. But the question of money is also about becoming a sustainable business. To that end, we've been growing our client base of advocacy organizations and trade associations that use the POPVOX Pro tools. Securing the first clients was probably the most challenging, since we were so new on the scene. But it has certainly gotten easier, and the early relationships we built are coming around as paid clients. *- Rachna Choudhry – Co-founding team, POPVOX*

It's ridiculously difficult to start a company and you're always faced with endless challenges, some of them so great that it seems insurmountable. But

I always say that most startups fail, not because their product or market sucks, or that they didn't get enough funding, but because they gave up too early or have co-founder issues. My three biggest challenges in starting a company were: (i) Hiring the right people who have the skills and entrepreneurial profile that we needed, but also equally passionate about the product we were building; (ii) Finding the right balance between iterating quickly via the 'lean startup' ways versus making a bet on a feature and spending a bit more time on it to make it super awesome; (iii) On a more personal note, how to find balance between over-working and establishing a healthy routine – if you and your employees get burnt out, it's bad for everyone. For example, we encourage everyone to work hard and be productive, but we also need to allocate enough time to work out and encourage healthy eating at the office during lunches. *- Cheryl Yeoh – Co-founder & CEO, Reclip.It (LaunchBox Digital and 500 Startups)*

Jessica Alba & Jesse Draper

Distribution was a major hurdle for us. YouTube wasn't working for me at the time and TV networks said I needed to grow my following before they would even consider doing anything with me, so I was in this Catch 22. My business partner Jonathan Polenz and I took nine months off from filming a whole season and did thirty-five distribution deals for the show, ranging from news sites to restaurants, and now we get two million aggregated views per video. *- Jesse Draper – Founder and Host, The Valley Girl Show*

**tastesavant**
——— *Food Discovery at Your Fingertips.* ———

My biggest challenge so far was finding a way to balance starting a family and starting my business. I just gave birth in early August to my beautiful baby boy and was pregnant over the course of the last year as I was building momentum on Taste Savant. It hasn't been easy managing both! While dealing with the emotional roller coaster of trying to grow a business, I was working on figuring out how I was going to try to have it all. But I managed to persevere and push (no pun intended) and I'm now with new life in my world and an exciting business to run. I learned to find strength in happy moments and high points to help carry me through the lows. And that is what helped me be more ready than ever to go for it all. Life could not be better, and I'm more prepared for harder challenges that may come my way. I actually now write for Forbes on this topic about being a woman entrepreneur and starting a family. *- Sonia Kapadia – Founder & CEO, Taste Savant*

*'It's one thing for your market to say they like what you're building, another for them to buy it.'*

Entering a market that's rapidly growing means both opportunity and rapid change. When you've thrown yourself completely into building and fundraising for a business, it's challenging to keep a constant eye on the market and the forces impacting it, and rapidly incorporate that information into your plans and actions. We had to develop the skills to plan, act, learn, adjust the team's actions and our pitch.

It's one thing for your market to say they like what you're building, another for them to buy it. Market research around a concept can yield valuable input and you have to do this. But then it's critical to get to a prototype, receive feedback from actual potential customers, and put what they say they'll pay for to the test. We went too far down the path of developing the platform before doing this, which cost us some time and re-work.

By definition, you have way too few resources and everyone's wearing multiple hats. The key is to know what you're good at, surround yourself with people who are really smart, able to play multiple roles, adaptable, and willing to do what it takes. It's normally worth paying for great talent, but that's often not feasible for a cash-strapped startup. If you have a compelling, high-potential idea and are making it happen, you can benefit from great talent without paying market rates.

Some executive roles can be filled with part-time people who have other income and will work for equity. We've paid a developer in India $13/hour for the same work that has cost $100/hour here. Advisors have contributed key inputs for free, and our talented student designer costs a fraction of a seasoned one. We've leveraged interns who worked for class credit, and volunteer help from at-home parents wanting to contribute their skills to our social good mission. Look realistically at your needs and be scrappy in finding all potential sources to fill them. *- Lynley Sides – Co-founder & CEO, The Glue Network (Springboard Enterprises accelerator)*

Naturally, as young founders we are learning along the way. But really any challenges we have come across turn out to be mini adventures in themselves that we've been able to learn and grow from. One challenge specifically has been to remember who we are and why we are doing this, and avoid being a 'business' for the sake of being a business. When we initially got funded, we made the mistake of acting like a business just because we got funded and not because it was the right time, or thing, to do. *- Garrett Gee – Co-founder, Scan.me (KickLabs)*

The problem with tackling hard problems is that they're inherently difficult. We started Leaky at MIT in the fall of 2010 with the plan to create a comparison engine by scraping insurance company websites and displaying rates on Leaky.com. We were accepted into Y-Combinator's summer 2011 batch on this premise, but when we launched in August 2011 we were shut down within four days by insurance companies' legal teams. We then went back to the drawing board and spent nearly eight months finding and building a workaround, which involved using publicly available insurance documents to reverse-engineer what an insurance company charges based on what they tell the government they would charge. This is how our auto insurance comparisons are done today. *- Jason Traff – Founder, Leaky (500 Startups)*

SALES – this is one of the toughest lessons I've learned over the past few years. Regardless of your product, market, target customers, etc., you will absolutely need to master the sales process and understand the core value you offer to customers and prove their willingness to pay. Everything else – product design, technology, team, equity etc. – is a distraction until you can prove that there is a core demand for the product or service you've proposed.

If I could start my career over again, I would have started first with an entry-level sales role in an organization or industry that I love (online video, for example). I speak from time to time on alumni panels about my startup experience and give this same advice to students preparing to graduate. They are always surprised at my suggestion to get a sales job out of college – 'Are you sure? I just want to start my own thing!' Unless you live in a vacuum, your 'own thing' will necessarily require customers and will exist in a marketplace with competing interests. Even if you're doing your 'own thing', sales is an absolutely critical element, without which everything else is for naught. *- Kieran Farr – Co-founder & CEO, VidCaster (500 Startups)*

There are a million little challenges that entrepreneurs face every single day. It never ends. For me, the biggest challenge was to transition away from the lure of 'easy' money building apps for clients, to becoming a 'single' product company. It's difficult because I was broke for a really long period of time while we validated the business idea and struggled to find the right time to move away from building someone else's dream to building my own. Something else that I found to be a challenge was the fact that we were from Adelaide. Don't get me wrong, I love the city, but the environment was not tech startup friendly at all. I remember trying to raise money very early on in Happy Inspector's life and not one single person in the local angel group was interested in putting a single dollar in. In Silicon Valley, it's a totally different story! The point I'm making is that being in the right place at the right time is very important. *- Jindou Lee – Founder, Happy Inspector (StartMate and 500 Startups)*

We didn't know what we didn't know. The technology space is noisy and it's hard to make sense of it all. You can spend weeks and months digging yourself into a rabbit hole on any of a hundred topics – all of which some thought leader will declare is absolutely vital. Playing the investor game, building an MVP, learning to code, the 'lean startup' movement, the 'lean startup is bullshit' movement ... it took us time to process and figure out our priorities. There was actually a long period where I vehemently denied that we were a 'tech startup' – we were just building a business with the plumbing handled by a website. Part of me actually still feels that way – so count me as naive or enlightened. *- Jay Lee – Co-founder & CEO, Smallknot (Techstars)*

We all know about the regular problems: teammates, funding, and perfection paralysis, but we want to talk about the huge impact your friends and family have. Understand that trying to get them to believe in your idea is tougher than it sounds (my mom still hasn't liked our Facebook page!) You also need to know that your startup life seeps into your relationships with friends and family, so be prepared for it and know that no matter how well you plan your work/life balance, it's always harder than you think. - *Young Han – Co-founder & CEO, GoVoluntr (500 Startups)*

Prioritizing. When you're just starting out and doing everything yourself from the menial to the critical, it's really difficult to stay focused on what's going to move the needle and make a meaningful difference between your company surviving or not. It can be extremely hard to see the forest through the trees, and to allocate your time to prioritize the most impactful activities first. Lately, I've been experimenting with writing the three most critical things that have to get done at the start of each day, which has been working well, but it's still very much a work in progress. - *Bernie Yoo – Co-founder, Bombfell (500 Startups)*

We made too many mistakes to count. One of the biggest was not building a network in Silicon Valley earlier. The Bay Area is the best place to raise capital by a long shot (not just my opinion, but that of most of the other founders I met through 500 and elsewhere that had moved from cities like Boston, Philadelphia etc.), and we spent a lot of time trying to raise capital in Seattle when we should have been focusing our attention in Silicon Valley. - *Nathan Parcells – Co-founder & CMO, InternMatch (500 Startups)*

## 'My mom still hasn't liked our Facebook page!'

On a general level, hiring the right people is always the most difficult challenge.

Specific to Nextdoor, building local community is tricky to get right, particularly replicating the social interactions that go on at the neighborhood level. Of course, we are far from declaring victory, and continue to face challenges every single day. That is what makes the experience so much fun! This challenge led us to spend a full year testing and tweaking the product before launching nationally. - *Nirav Tolia – Founder & CEO, Nextdoor*

In the beginning it was difficult for us to transition from client work to building our own product. Initially we were horrible at pitching our idea. Instead of focusing on the big vision, we'd talk about the product's features, because that's what we were used to doing. It was also a new experience for us to take the product to market; we were used to building something then handing it off to the client. - *Katrina Brickner – Co-founder, Marquee (Techstars)*

One of the biggest challenges we've had is building a technology company and raising money in Boise, Idaho. We have all seen and experienced the tremendous environment that exists in places like Silicon Valley and Boulder, but unfortunately the community in Boise is still very nascent, and there was a lot less communal support than we would have experienced elsewhere. We all love Boise and the people here, don't get me wrong, but it certainly added to the challenge of being an early-stage startup.

Also, our lack of food service industry experience was a big hang-up for some investors. Understandably so as it's a huge, complex industry, but it is also the reason why we've been able to do what we've done. We saw inefficiencies that seasoned food service veterans did not, and that was the catalyst for our business. We've since recruited a number of food service professionals to serve in an advisory role, and this has gone a long way towards both quieting our critics and helping in the development of our business model. - *Wink Jones – Co-founder & CEO, Mealticket (Techstars)*

I left my job working on the Amazon Kindle to start a dating company and some of my friends thought I was crazy. I didn't have any money so I had to find free ways to eat and sleep. - *Nick Soman – Founder & CEO, LikeBright (Techstars)*

When they say startups are a roller coaster, they're really not kidding. For a while I was a single founder, which is incredibly tough – there's nobody else around who's as passionate and committed as you are, so you have to ride the good and the bad out without a good feedback loop to keep yourself sane. We also nearly ran out of money a couple of months after Boomerang's launch. Between server expenses, keeping ourselves fed and sheltered, and our difficulty raising money in Boston, we got really close to the wire before we took a very fortunate car ride. - *Alex Moore – Founder & CEO, Baydin (Techstars)*

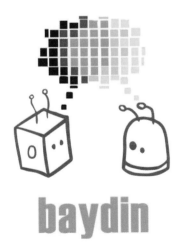

*'If I could start my career over again, I would have started first with an entry-level sales role in an organization or industry that I love.'*

Keen is admittedly in an unsexy area. So while all sorts of consumer Internet nonsense was getting money thrown at it, we had an uphill battle raising initial funds. Inside the industry, we still deal with large partners who just can't shake their out-of-date, OEM approach. But we've made a decision early on that we are going to stick to our vision and only do deals that support it. After consistently getting industry recognition, starting at our launch at Graph Expo 2011 (where we won an award) and our recent 2012 InterTech Technology Award (Keen is the youngest company in its 34-year history), we are now getting very well known. - *Vitaly Golomb – Founder & CEO, Keenprint*

The gaming industry is classically defined as a hits-driven business. We struggled with this early on when we had just one game in development. Folks would ask, 'Are you creating an app or a company?' Since then we've created our own game engine that powers these reality driven games and we have multiple games in the pipeline. We are now a fully fledged gaming company. The lesson here is that you must be able to articulate what you will become before you get there. - *Dave Bisceglia – Co-founder & CEO, The Tap Lab (Techstars)*

Knowing when to scale and where to focus is difficult. We thought we had a product to scale into the Enterprise over a year ago and it turned out we were wrong. Our first Enterprise customer showed us what we were missing. At the time we tried to be both an Enterprise and SMB product. We learned that you have to focus in the early days. We stopped major development on our SMB product shortly after learning this new lesson and now the SMB product gets new features that also make sense for Enterprise. As we mature, we will expand on our SMB product, but it will focus on that market instead of trying to please multiple crowds. Fight one battle at a time early on and you will do a better job. *- Rob Lenderman – Co-founder & CIO, and David Greenbaum – Co-founder & CEO, BoostCTR (500 Startups)*

Don't assume you know how your co-founders are feeling about something; it's hugely important to over communicate, find healthy ways of dealing with conflict, and making sure you're aligned, expectations-wise around the business. I had an earlier startup fail because of founder issues, and I think it's one of the biggest causes of failure for startups. *- Todd Silverstein – Co-founder & CEO, Vizify (Techstars)*

## 'You're either addressing problems or ignoring them.'

Start everything earlier. Startups have a finite timeline, at least until they get profitable, and our ability to move quickly is one of our biggest assets. This means that you've got to do everything fast. Plan ahead, test hypotheses relentlessly, and proactively seek out problems to fix. Like one of our investors said, 'You're either addressing problems or ignoring them.' You should never put off a difficult phone call, writing an awkward email or trying to close a business deal because, in a startup, you don't have the luxury of time. *- Jason Traff – Founder, Leaky (500 Startups)*

My co-founder left the company last December. I have no regrets launching this company with him – in fact, it would have been impossible without him

and he remains a good friend. However, I should have trusted my gut and had a conversation with him sooner to find out if he was still happy with his role in the company. There were probably six months where he could have been creating more value elsewhere, and we could have brought in someone more energized to fill his role. I was afraid to have this difficult conversation, not knowing if I could keep the business going without him. Turns out it was a very positive change for everyone involved. *- Ken Johnson – Co-founder, Manpacks (Seed Funded by 500 Startups)*

Don't always work on the things that are technologically the most intriguing. Do a little research ahead of time to be sure that users actually want what you're going to build, and that you can actually deliver a good product. We spent a vast amount of resources building an offline mode for Lucidchart, only to find that the browser support was spotty and the user demand was much lower than we expected. We've since dropped support for the feature entirely. *- Karl Sun – Co-founder & CEO, and Ben Dilts – Co-founder & CTO, Lucidchart (500 Startups)*

## 'I didn't know how many times we would start from scratch.'

I didn't build enough buffer into the amount of money I thought I needed to raise when I started. I didn't take into account all the mistakes, prototypes and code that would be thrown out. I didn't know how many times we would start from scratch. Knowing what I know now, I would have built those assumptions into my expected launch timeline and my financial projections. Rookie move. *- Maxine Manafy – Co-founder & CEO, Bunndle (500 Startups)*

Mixime Manafy

Our first startup idea was a 'Daily Candy for Dating' concept where we profiled one single person in the city and emailed it out to everyone. We were making an assumption that people would forward along emails about people like they do about restaurants, and lead to organic signups that way. But we spent months designing and building stuff before actually launching – at which point we discovered that assumption was way wrong – when we could have discovered that without building anything and just using Mailchimp and Google Surveys. With Bombfell, we built nothing until we gained confidence that our core assumptions were holding up. *- Bernie Yoo – Co-founder, Bombfell (500 Startups)*

## 'Make sure you hire slowly and fire quickly.'

My co-founder Frank and I had another startup before PayByGroup, during which we made a lot of first-timer mistakes. One that applies to everyone: make sure you hire slowly and fire quickly. *- Camilo Acosta – Co-founder & CEO, PayByGroup (500 Startups)*

#1 lesson would be to identify real users or customers for your product. Early adopters tend to get excited about anything, but you want to find people who need your solution that bad that they are willing to pay for it. *- Khuram Hussain, Founder & CEO, Fileboard (500 Startups)*

We make mistakes all the time and, of course, that's all part of our learning process. The only big mistakes we feel bad about are the ones we don't correct, where we know something's bad or not working and it takes a while to take decisive action to fix it. Along this journey, one of the best lessons has been to trust our instincts and take decisive action when we know it's needed. *- Adam Bonnifield – Co-founder, Spinnakr (500 Startups)*

Startups are marathons, not sprints. You will have more down days than up, but determination, will and strength can take you far if you are willing to dig in and execute. In terms of mistakes and lessons, here are some of the top things I have learned:

1. There is no silver bullet. There is not a single deal that can make your company. Don't look at a deal as the endgame to the startup, but rather as a means to a specific milestone that is in the near future.
2. Customers will always frustrate you. The key to dealing with customers is to respond to everyone, but have a strong rule of authority.
3. Having the right team is more important than the right vision. It takes a system of people working well together and are passionate about a problem or idea to produce consistently great results. *- Ryan Stoner – Co-founder & CEO, MoPix (500 Startups)*

We bootstrapped the company initially by doing individual test prep tutoring. It paid the bills and provided us with some great user research, but it was emotionally draining and highly distracting. While we initially didn't want to raise money, we discovered that we could move much faster if the software business was our dominant focus. We still teach a few hours a week to stay in touch with our users, but it's much less than we did when we needed to teach for our living. *- Miro Kazakoff - Co-founder & CEO, and Tom Rose – Co-founder & CPO, Testive (Techstars)*

We probably held on to our initial business plan for too long before making the pivot into what we're doing now. I think if we had been more open to it and really listened to the market, we might have made this change sooner and would now be further along in our development. Bottom line is to always be talking to one's users and make sure that what's being built is actually useful and usable.

*- Wink Jones – Co-founder & CEO, Mealticket (Techstars)*

Wink Jones

148

Besides occasionally omitting the oxford comma, I would say hiring. Don't hire who's available, wait to get someone great. If you think you can't afford someone great, find a way to attract them with something you do have. Engineers like to work with smart people on hard problems. Designers (and I am one) are little Napoleons who want to call the shots and be heard ... and, by the way, with good reason, since we are taught to articulate and solve problems. Marketing/Sales/BD people want a kick-ass product that sells itself. *- Vitaly Golomb – Founder & CEO, Keenprint (Funded by 500 Startups)*

One of my favorite quotes is from legendary coach John Wooden: 'If you're not making mistakes, then you're not doing anything. I'm positive that a doer makes mistakes.'

I've tried to do a lot of things and so I've made many mistakes – too many to list here. But I am focused on learning from them and not repeating them – I think that in itself is the most important

learning. *- Nirav Tolia – founder & CEO, Nextdoor*

## 'Designers (and I am one) are little Napoleons.'

One of our biggest mistakes was not moving to New York sooner. While in Miami, we worked in our own office and rarely interacted with people within the same industry. We also have a habit of waiting until things are 'perfect' before launching, which causes us to miss out on valuable early user feedback. That's why immediately after Techstars we forced ourselves to launch an alpha of our product, bugs and all. *- Katrina Brickner – Co-founder, Marquee (Techstars)*

One of the biggest mistakes we made was not starting our company while we were in college at Boston University. We had the idea and all of the resources to start building. In fact, it was the perfect environment to start a company. But, we waited until after graduation to begin. Why? Because we were scared. We wanted to focus on our GPAs and our collegiate social lives. Lesson: that's stupid. Don't do that. Start now! *- Dave Bisceglia – Co-founder & CEO, The Tap Lab (Techstars)*

## 'The only big mistakes we feel bad about are the ones we don't correct.'

It took me a couple of weeks to come to grips with the fact that things needed to change. It's really easy to get into a stubborn, prideful trap. This is especially true when there are signs that things are working. Nobody wants to hear that their baby isn't perfect. The quicker you can come to grips and the faster you can iterate, the better off you'll be.

When you make the decision to change, make it with 100% conviction. Communicate clearly and

don't apologize. After all, the reason you change
is to make something better. Don't half-ass it.
*- Dana Severson – Co-founder & CEO, Chasm.*
*io (AngelPad)*

'If you're not making
mistakes, then
you're not doing
anything.'

– John Wooden

ACCELERATE

STAR
ADVI

TUP
CE

# STARTUP
# ADVICE

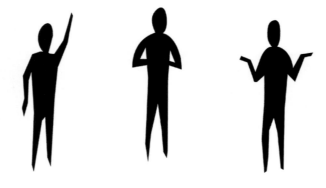

Charlie Munger, Vice Chairman of Berkshire Hathaway and "right-hand man" to Warren Buffet, explained in his 1986 Harvard commencement speech that if you want a prescription for guaranteed misery in life, then "try to learn everything you possibly can from your own personal experience, minimizing what you learn vicariously from the good and bad experience of others, living, and dead. This is a sure-shot producer of misery and second-rate achievement." Use advice as a way to stand on the shoulders of giants so you won't have to jump so high.

If you embark on a startup adventure, the final destination will always be a guess and the journey will most definitely be treacherous—only experienced explorers know of the pirates and reefs that await, and even those cannot predict all obstacles. This is the nature of a startup. In this journey some routes may detour you, set you back, or nearly capsize your "ship." So, if there's a captain of another ship who's embarked on a comparable journey, it's in the name of good sense to drink rum and share stories. This does not mean you should forfeit your leadership by rigidly following someone else's advice, but their advice should be part the compass that guides you.

In this chapter, entrepreneurs share their thoughts and experiences on starting a company. Consider their advice as something that could help you avoid misery in your startup life. To start, I'd like to share some principles that I have found to be helpful:

1) Study – actively work to increase your industry IQ, read as much as possible, and have passion for your subject. Set yourself up to be an authority in your field.

2) Listen more than you speak – you don't learn much when your mouth is open.

3) Ask for help – don't be afraid or embarrassed to ask a question or get something wrong. The only unforgivable mistakes are ones that we had the chance to avoid, but chose not to for the sake of pride.

4) Give more than you take – always think about how you can help others. Be a connector, a supporter, and a resource, not because you expect something in return but simply because you take joy in helping others.

5) Take pride in your work.

Here are my top three pieces of advice:

1. Take all advice lightly: think deeply about all advice before you act upon it. I've seen several companies become derailed after a notable person gave advice that they blindly followed. While the advice might be valid, it is important that you think deeply about all major decisions that you make for your company. What was true last year isn't necessarily true today, and what worked for another company may not work for your company.
2. Solve a pain point you understand. It makes everything easier.
3. Talking to customers is great, but requires skill. Take the time to learn how to ask the right questions and create learning plans.

And a bonus:
4. If you feel like you're outside your comfort zone, you're probably doing something right. Embrace that feeling. *- Brett Hellman – CEO, hall (AngelPad)*

Take charge of your product, if you don't know how to code and you have a technology company, learn. Understanding how to code enables you to not just get started with a prototype, but also be on top of development during the early stages.

Always remember that those people that want your product will pay for it. Don't be scared to charge. I don't believe in giving a product away for free, even as a test. Giving your product away for free will only get the wrong people testing it and the people that you want using it will probably not give the product their full attention because they are not committed monetarily to their decision. I am not saying charge full price to those looking to test your product, but charge enough to force them to commit to testing it thoroughly. *- David Buxton – Founder, Arachnys (Springboard)*

First, I would recommend picking an idea where it is, at least in theory, possible to make money from day one. The faster you have people making the decision – 'Should I pay these guys money or not?' – the better. We didn't do that and things turned out okay, but I think this was more luck than anything.

Second, I will repeat the common startup advice: release an MVP (Minimum Viable Product) as soon as you possibly can. Time spent before actually launching is time spent in an illusory magical world where self-delusion is all too easy.

Third, if you are a technical founder, be very, very careful about writing too much code. I am a programmer, and I am susceptible to this. It's fun to write code, and it's fun to add more and more features to your product. But it's also only one of a number of extremely important things to be doing.

I'd even go as far as to say that it might be good to periodically take a week off from coding to devote to other things, just to make sure they actually get done – things like sales, marketing, user testing, etc. I've seen far too many founders work endless hours coding and adding more and more features, while leaving aside simple things like user testing that would do far more for their businesses. *- Mike Turitzin – Co-founder, WorkFlowy (Y Combinator)*

*'If you feel like you're outside your comfort zone, you're probably doing something right.'*

You can't go it alone. If there's one thing Springboard confirmed it's that building a strong support network is vital to the success of early-stage businesses; indeed, any stage business. Get out there and meet people who can open doors for you. There's a lot of noise in the startup space, but broadly most people are happy to help where they can and redirect you where they can't – make use of 'entrepreneur's empathy'!

Secondly, find a way to galvanise your thoughts and efforts and start moving forward. For us the catalyst came in the form of the business plan we wrote for that competition back at university. Beyond the prize money we won and the contacts we made, it forced us to actually act, to flesh out the idea we had and get a move on turning it into a business. On this note, I would also say that, while a business plan is useful for articulating and documenting strategies and roadmaps, be prepared to deviate from it! Inevitably you're going to duck and dive, chop and change, and you'll do so often in order to give your company the best chance of success.

It's often said that the business you end up with will be very different from the idea you started with. We're only part of the way there, but already we're heading in exciting new directions and loving every second of it. - *Patrick Elliott – Co-founder, Backscratchers (Springboard)*

Starting a new company often requires that you quit your existing job, enter a new (potentially unexplored) space, and pick up a skillset you're not familiar with. All of these can be extremely daunting, as you're ultimately leaving your comfort zone. I follow three pieces of advice around taking such a leap, ensuring I'm moving forward and keeping myself honest:

1. Set clear, quantifiable metrics for success. I set a personal sales target for year one of Canopy Labs, both to force myself to learn how to sell, and to ensure our product was worthy of selling. We surpassed our targets and we feel great about where we are.

2. Start every week by listing the four or five challenges you're facing, with a list of two or three things you can do to overcome them. This makes it easy to deal with your biggest fears, but also ensures you have a plan of action for your most important things to do.

3. Finally, have someone you can rant to every day. Be it your wife, parents, best friend, or anyone who will listen. It's good to vent and allows you to become a bit more rational once you cool off.

When starting Canopy Labs, one of my mentors told me that: 'Success in business requires a personal transformation.' I truly believe that the success of your startup is dependent on how effective you are as a leader, planner, product developer, and sales person.

Results-driven people who overcome challenges rationally and quickly will do well in startups – with or without an accelerator. Such a mindset will help you get into whichever programs are right for you. - *Wojciech Gryc – Co-founder & CEO, Canopy Labs (Y Combinator)*

Be flexible and open to new ideas. Don't get too stuck on the concept you started out with and be ready to make a pivot if you need to. If your idea sucks or just doesn't receive the feedback you thought it would, you may find yourself throwing everything out and starting over before finishing the program. - *Wink Jones – Co-founder & CEO, Mealticket (Techstars)*

1. Surround yourself with great people.

2. Build something that people really want.

3. Let the journey be the reward. Getting funding and, more importantly, building a successful company is an incredibly difficult challenge. Entrepreneurs experience the highest of highs and the lowest of lows. If you don't love this roller coaster, starting a company is not for you. - *Nirav Tolia – Founder & CEO, Nextdoor*

Focus on your team. The team is, hands down, the most important asset you have as a company. Building a startup is very hard and you can't do it without great people. There are a lot of ups and downs. You need to make sure your team, and especially your co-founder/s, are going to be ready for that.

You'll find out that you can't raise money for another year. Make sure your co-founder will stick by you. You'll be tested and find out all your weaknesses (and strengths!). You'll create something and find out no one wants to use it. You'll work on something for months, only to find out you went down the wrong path. *- Hany Rashwan – Founder & CEO, Ribbon (AngelPad)*

The single most important thing is customer development because it doesn't matter how great you think your ideas is, or how much awesome advice you receive and networking you do, the only person that should ever really matter to you is the person that is going to use your product. *- Alex Depledge – Co-founder, Hassle (Springboard)*

Make sure that you'd be happy working on whatever problem you're trying to solve for many years to come. Obviously, you have to work incredibly hard and have depths of determination to draw upon. In the meantime, try to devour as much knowledge as you can from people who have already been there and done it. *- Julian Keenaghan – Co-founder, Tastebuds.fm (Springboard)*

Start working on small side projects while you're at school, or at your job, or whatever you're currently doing. Try to get little things out there and off the ground, and, if you can, even start making a bit of money. It doesn't have to be anything major – but if you just leap head first into starting a company without having even made a website or talking to a hundred users, you might make a ton of unnecessary mistakes. *- Ajay Meht – Co-founder, FamilyLeaf (Y Combinator)*

*'If you really want to start a company, the only thing that matters is actually doing it.'*

Do it. Building a company is one of the more difficult and challenging things you'll be likely to do, and most businesses will fail. It's also one of the most rewarding and exciting things you can do. Take the time to truly understand the risks involved and to have a rough idea of what you want to build. But, if you really want to start a company, the only thing that matters is actually doing it. *- Ryan Nielsen – Co-founder, Tumult (Y Combinator)*

*'Build the right team.'*

It's hard starting a company with a team, but even harder alone. Build the right team. Surround yourself with people who believe in your idea and in you. There are a lot of naysayers out there and it's really important to shield yourself from that. This doesn't mean ignoring potential problems, competitors and devil's advocate's that can help you improve your product or direction, but don't get discouraged easily. It's not always the idea most of the time, it's the person behind the idea and the execution. There were hundreds of social networks before Facebook and hundreds of ecommerce platforms before eBay. The difference

Julian Keenaghan

between the failures and successes is often the team and the execution. *- Vanessa Dawson – founder, Evry*

Pick a business you're truly passionate about. It's tempting to work on something only because it looks like a huge opportunity with tons of money to be made. But this is hard – mentally, physically, and emotionally – so if you don't truly love what you're doing, you'll burn out. *- Alex Tryon, – Founder & CEO, Artsicle*

Make sure that the opportunity is worth it: So many entrepreneurs start businesses because of business lust. They become intoxicated with an idea, but don't think through the scope of the opportunity. If you are going to risk your time, money and effort, make sure that the pay-off – whether financial or qualitative – is big enough to justify your actual costs and opportunity costs.

Give yourself enough runway: businesses can take two to three years to get a solid foundation. I have a 'Rule of Three' in business: it will take three times as long, be three times as costly, and be three times as challenging as you expect it will be. So, make sure that you have enough money to start the business, operate the business, and live on for at least two years. Look, if it has taken Oprah – who has more connections, capital and fans than just about anyone – a couple of years to get her new network under way, it'll probably take you at least the same.

Test it out: if there's a way to get experience or test your business out on a small scale before diving in with both feet, do it. Test the viability, see if you still enjoy it over long periods of time, see what customer feedback is, etc. This will give you important feedback to adapt or tweak your model if needed, or perhaps realize that you might be barking up the wrong tree *- Carol Roth – Media pundit and best selling author of The Entrepreneur Equation*

I have two pieces of advice: 1) Follow through and 2) Be likable.

Follow through, because that is how you move forward, gain trust, and gain respect. When you start your first company, the people around you are crucial in giving you that kick start. When you demonstrate that you can get things done, these people will support you. When mentors see that you are executing the plans, they become more interested in helping you.

Be likable, for similar reasons as mentioned above. There are many ways to be likable; you can be thoughtful, be punctual, be sincere, be awesome. One example I can think of is that entrepreneurs sometimes think only of their own businesses and forget to care for other people and their businesses. I guess when you think about your business 24/7, it's easy to fall into this trap. So take a step back and make sure you're not being an ass! *- Tanya Huang – Founder, Knot Theory*

Firstly, I think such a huge factor is attitude. So many people are put off from executing their ideas because of the fear of failing. I can personally say I've made a lot of mistakes, but it's about dusting yourself off and having the determination to battle through it all and come out with a great product and business.

The next big thing is advice. It's really important to find people around you and your business who you can trust and that know their stuff. There is so much to do starting up your own business that having a few more experienced eyes and ears around your business can make all the difference. I'd also say don't fall into the trap of thinking you know everything and thinking you're always right, and that's why having good people around you with the right experience is so worth it. Even with a business plan, having experienced people around can give you a much better idea on time frames and roadmaps is really valuable, the next challenge is actually listening.

The more work and planning you can put into your business, the better things will go. Nothing is ever certain in a startup and things are changing all the time, but having a clear plan and strategy for your business will certainly put you in a strong position.

Finally, it's about staying calm and enjoying yourself. Get ready for a massive roller coaster of emotions. - *Dom Lewis – Co-founder, Tray.io (Springboard)*

First and foremost, you should find people who are in the industry you are interested in and start building relationships. Relationships take a long time to develop, so you should start early by asking them smart questions, meeting them if possible, and picking their brain about anything you can. It's hard to understate how important these relationships can become as your business begins to move forward. - *Nathan Parcells – Co-founder & CMO, InternMatch (500 Startups)*

1) Find an area of the world that you are instinctively excited and curious about. Not what you are reading about in the news that the world has already deemed exciting (because by then it's too late). Music analytics was not something people were asking or searching for several years ago – we are creating a new market. If I had pitched Big Data for the music industry four years ago, no one would have understood what we did each day at NextBigSound. Rather than getting more routine, it gets more interesting as we go down the rabbit hole gathering more data, signing on more customers, understanding their questions better, and providing answers which lead to more questions. This is only possible because of our innate curiosity and excitement about finding the truth in this arena.

2) Start talking with as many other people as you possibly can about your idea and the part of the world you are most interested in. You never know who has a cousin/friend/classmate who shares a similar fascination and you want to expose yourself to as much serendipity as humanly possible. The famous saying is: 'It's not what you know, it's who you know.' I don't think that's entirely right. I think it's more about who knows you. If you are the guy always talking about geo-location ten years before it's all over TechCrunch or the person obsessed with photography five years before the sale of Instagram makes headlines, opportunities will find you.

3) Once you've found the sector and others who share your enthusiasm, it's time to run as fast as you possibly can. This means real validated learning with customers and users. In the early days, don't be too obsessed with A/B testing (since you have no users this will take weeks to run and provide questionable data), build a product, put it in front of people, get their feedback, rinse and repeat. At NextBigSound we are twenty-two people and still trying to speed these cycles up no matter the cost. We moved the entire company from Boulder to New York City to be able to put new product in front of end customers in the music industry in half the time from when we were in Boulder. These cycles can never be fast enough.

While these three things are my advice for an entrepreneur looking to build a massive, industry defining company, funnily enough it is the same advice I would give to those looking to get into an accelerator. At the end of the day, they are looking for a team of people working in an area they are incredibly excited about that can move at lightening speed towards building their product and business. - *Alex White – Co-founder & CEO, NextBigSound (Techstars)*

*'Starting a company is like throwing yourself off the cliff and assembling an airplane on the way down.'*

- Reid Hoffman, Founder of LinkedIn

Schedule quality time with your co-founders. Steve and I went to our favorite pub and got a beer together every other week or so. Just like married couples need to schedule date night, startup founders need to schedule down time. You'll already be spending more time with your co-founder than with your significant other, but most of that time is taking care of your baby, so you need to block out time to take care of each other. If you don't plan for that time, you won't get it and it will slowly kill you and your business.

Assuming you accept a spot in an accelerator and make it through to demo day, here's what's going to happen: you're going to get sick. Like cannot get off the couch, do not want to be alive ill. As soon as the stress release happens, your body is going to shut down. Having sat in the Techstars Seattle co-working space for three batches of startups, I can tell you that it happens to everyone. *- Steve Krenzel and Brandon Bloom - Co-founders, Thinkfuse (Techstars)*

Enjoy it and make sure you take time to celebrate the victories

When you get your first paying customer, take the team out to dinner. Have a company outing when you build the first 'sticky' thing you put together. Remember that most folks never even get to the point of starting something, so really relish moving past that point. *- Alex Moore – Founder & CEO, Baydin (Techstars)*

Brandon Bloom

'*Make sure you take time to celebrate the victories.*'

# SELECT TOPICS

## Evaluating a Buyout Offer:

There's a lot to think about and it's a complicated process. Even if you want to run your startup forever and turn it into a giant freestanding company, like we're doing at HubSpot, keep an eye on who you are valuable to, who you threaten, and who competes with those you are threatening to disrupt. It's a big part of your job as founder to know where you stand and to whom you are valuable. This is because companies don't get sold, they get bought. You can't 'push' a rope on an acquisition, you have to have something people want and are willing to go through the hassle of acquiring and integrating your company. Also, don't get distracted by acquisition offers— they can be a dime a dozen and, frequently, meaningless. You just go keep building value, and in the end you will have something valuable to someone. *- Laura Fitton – Founder, oneforty, and author of Twitter for Dummies. Currently Inbound Marketing Evangelist at HubSpot*

## ROE *vs* ROI

Like anything else, being an authority takes time and effort. So, you have to ask yourself why you are doing it and if it's the best way for you to achieve your business goals. Sometimes you end up with more of what I call 'ROE' (return on ego) than 'ROI' (return on investment).

The one thing about being an authority is that you can raise your awareness and maybe even your fees, but the secret is in leveraging your status. Most people think that they will get more business from just being quoted or appearing on TV. That isn't usually the case. It's what you do with that exposure, which, of course, takes more time and effort! *- Carol Roth – Media pundit and best selling author of The Entrepreneur Equation*

## A Story of a Startup's Early Stages

We had created the VidCaster platform as a side project while working on VidSF, a local online video TV station serving the San Francisco Bay Area. We were very lucky that customers began to approach us about using this software for their own purposes. We hadn't considered making VidCaster available externally—this took us by considerable surprise that other folks would want to use our internal tool for their own projects. This was our first lesson in listening to customer input to validate the product and drive further improvements. Before taking the plunge and pivoting away from local TV, we reached out to our personal network of friends working in startups, small businesses and larger organizations such as universities to get anecdotal input on the usefulness of such a solution. We didn't perform traditional market research, but we did buy our friends beers to get input on the problems they had with online video distribution and how to measurably drive sales goals through video marketing.

After this input from prospective customers and our 'market research' with our personal network, we decided to fully pivot in 2010 to offer VidCaster as a standalone solution for businesses to distribute and measure video content marketing. We were lucky enough to be able to work with Airbnb and Indiana University as our initial beta customers. They served as both our initial clients and a sounding board for iterating the feature sets that would be valuable for them and for exploring pricing options.

In 2011 we began to actively market and sell VidCaster to startups and technology companies in the Bay Area, such as Zendesk, Twilio, and Microsoft. This helped us get a feel for pricing, use cases, and how to pitch this to a wider market. We also began to see the potential size of this opportunity – we learned that almost every business struggles with their video marketing strategy, especially proving the ROI or effectiveness of those efforts. This began

'Limited life experience + overgeneralization = Advice.'

- Paul Buchheit

to light our fire to start raising funding, which is what led us to join the 500 Startups accelerator in Mountain View. *- Kieran Farr – Co-founder & CEO, VidCaster (500 Startups)*

## Validating Big Industry Demand

The printing industry is immense. We are betting on a major paradigm shift in the way it does business. Timing for a major shift in behavior has to be driven by a trend. There were a number of companies that brought ecommerce to this industry over the years, but it's only now going mainstream (primary way of doing business) because of the following factors: general acceptance and preference for ecommerce on the buyer/end-customer side; broadband penetration and ease of large-file transfer (people forget that only 10% of the population had broadband connections ten years ago); and secular industry pressure to streamline operations and cost structures. Certainly we had the benefit of knowing our industry on a deep level, but keeping up with economic data and trends is something I take very seriously. There are a number of research organizations and think tanks that operate in the graphic arts/printing space which we track and gather data from regularly. In fact, we like numbers so much that we put together an infographic campaign that went viral: printisbig.com *- Vitaly Golomb – Founder & CEO, Keenprint*

## Pivoting

We had a lot of false/positive signals with Wahooly. Our users loved the concept, the media loved the concept, and investors loved the concept. The problem was, love for an idea doesn't always translate into a motivated user base. When we stepped back and took the time to talk to our users and customers, it was clear that we had missed the mark on what everyone truly wanted.In influence marketing, the common logic is that rewards need to be monetary. However, what we discovered is that those who are creating the greatest impact in social

are more concerned with reputation, credibility, and exposure. Incentivizing with rewards, cash and equity had a reverse effect on our model.

Once it was clear that our assumptions were incorrect, it was obvious that a shift needed to occur. Our biggest asset this time around was that we had a group of 1,500 users who told us what they wanted. That's about as easy as it gets. *- Dana Severson – Co-founder & CEO, Chasm.io (AngelPad)*

> *'Love for an idea doesn't always translate into a motivated user.'*

# THE ACCE
## LI

LERATOR

ST

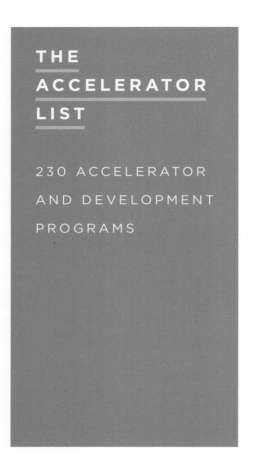

# THE ACCELERATOR LIST

## 230 ACCELERATOR AND DEVELOPMENT PROGRAMS

**Wayra**
**Argentina**
Web technologies, Software, Mobile-web, Gaming and e-Commerce
$30,000-70,000 | 10%
wayra.org/en

**Anz Innovyz Start**
**Australia | Adelaide**
Web technologies, Software, Mobile-web, Gaming and e-Commerce
AU $20000 | 8%
innovyzstart.com

**StartMate**
**Australia | Sydney**
Web technologies, Software, Mobile-web, Gaming and e-Commerce
AU $50,000 | 7%
startmate.com.au

**Founder Institute**
**Belgium**
Web technologies, Software, Mobile-web, Gaming and e-Commerce
3.5%
founderinstitute.com

**Wayra**
**Brazil**
Web technologies, Software, Mobile-web, Gaming and e-Commerce
$30,000-70,000 | 10%
wayra.org/en

**Flow Ventures**
**Canada | Montreal**
Web technologies, Software, Mobile-web, Gaming and e-Commerce
flowventures.com

**FounderFuel**
**Canada | Montreal**
Web technologies, Software, Mobile-web, Gaming and e-Commerce
$50000 | 9%
founderfuel.com

### Nxtp.labs
**Argentina | Buenos Aires**
Spanish-speaking technology, Web
technologies, Software, Mobile-web,
Gaming and e-Commerce
$25000 | 2-10%
nxtplabs.net

### Citrix Startup Accelerator
**Australia**
Web technologies, Software
$20,000 - $400,000
citrixStartupaccelerator.com

### Angelcube
**Australia | Melbourne**
Web technologies, Software, Mobile-
web, Gaming and e-Commerce
AU $20,000 | 10%
angelcube.com.au

### Pollenizer
**Australia, NSW**
Web technologies, Software, Mobile-
web, Gaming and e-Commerce
pollenizer.com

### Pushstart Accelerator
**Australia | Sydney**
Web and Mobile
AU $20,000 | 8%
pushstart.com.au/about

### Nest'up
**Belgium, Mont-Saint-Guibert**
Web technologies, Software, Mobile-
web, Gaming and e-Commerce
nestup.be

### Eleven Startup Accelerator
**Bulgaria, Sofia**
Web technologies, Software, Mobile-web,
Gaming and e-Commerce
€50,000
eleven.bg

### LAUNCHub
**Bulgaria, Sofia**
Web technologies, Software, Mobile-
web, Gaming and e-Commerce
€30000 | 8 -10%
launchub.com

### Extreme Startups
**Canada, Toronto**
Web technologies, Software, Mobile-
web, Gaming and e-Commerce
$50000 | 10%
extremeStartups.com

### Extreme Venture
### Partners University
**Canada, Toronto**
Web technologies, Software, Mobile-web, Gaming and
e-Commerce
$5,000 Per founder | 10%
extremevp.com/university

**Jolt**
**Canada, Toronto**
Web technologies, Software, Mobile-
web, Gaming and e-Commerce
$50,000 | 9%
jolt.marsdd.com

**GrowLab**
**Canada, Vancover**
Web technologies, Software, Mobile-
web, Gaming and e-Commerce
$25,000 | 5-9%
growlab.ca

**Wayra**
**Chile**
Web technologies, Software, Mobile-
web, Gaming and e-Commerce
$30,000-70,000 | 10%
wayra.org/en

**China Accelerator**
**China - Dalian, Lanong**
Web technologies, Software, Mobile-
web, Gaming and e-Commerce
$30,000-70,000 | 10%
wayra.org/en

**HAXLR8R**
**China, Shenzhen**
Hardware
$25,000 | 8%
haxlr8r.com

**Wayra**
**Colombia**
Web technologies, Software, Mobile-
web, Gaming and e-Commerce
$30,000-70,000 | 10%
wayra.org/en

**StartupYard**
**Czech Republic, Prague**
Web technologies, Software, Mobile-
web, Gaming and e-Commerce
$10,000 | 10%
Startupyard.cz

**Startup Bootcamp**
**Denmark, Copenhagen**
Web technologies, Software, Mobile-
web, Gaming and e-Commerce
€15,000 | 8%
Startupbootcamp.org

**Vigo**
**Finland**
Internationally focused Web technologies,
Software, Mobile-web, Gaming and e-Commerce
€1-2 million
vigo.fi

**Startup Sauna**
**Finland**
Web technologies, Software, Mobile-
web, Gaming and e-Commerce
€1,000 - €20,000
Startupsauna.com

**Communitech Hyperdrive**
**Canada, Waterloo**
Web technologies, Software, Mobile-web,
Gaming and e-Commerce
$40,000 - $55,000 | 6.4%
hyperdrive.communitech.ca

**RYERSON Futures**
**Canada, Toronto**
Web technologies, Software, Mobile-
web, Gaming and e-Commerce
Up to $50,000 | 5-10%
ryersonfutures.com

**Lightspeed
Venture Partners**
**China, Shanghai**
Consumer, enterprise technology and
cleantech
lsvp.com

**Innovation Works**
**China - Shanghai, Beijing**
Web technologies, Software, Mobile-
web, Gaming and e-Commerce
en.chuangxin.com

**TechSquare**
**Czech Republic**
Web technologies, Software, Mobile-
web, Gaming and e-Commerce
techsquare.cz/en

**Wayra**
**Czech Republic**
Web technologies, Software, Mobile-
web, Gaming and e-Commerce
$30,000-70,000 | 10%
wayra.org/en

**Flat6 Labs**
**Egypt, Giza**
Web technologies, Software, Mobile-web,
Gaming and e-Commerce
EGP 60,000-75,000 | 10-15%
flat6labs.com

**Wise Guys**
**Estonia, Tallinn**
Web technologies, Software, Mobile-web,
Gaming and e-Commerce
€5.000 per founder (max €15.000) | 8%
Startupwiseguys.com

**Summer of Startup**
**Finland, Helsinki**
Web technologies, Software, Mobile-
web, Gaming and e-Commerce
€5000 per founder
summerofStartups.com

**BoostTurku**
**Finland, Turku**
Web technologies, Software, Mobile-web,
Gaming and e-Commerce
€4,000 per founder
boostturku.com/sos

ACCELERATE

### Founder Institute
**France**

Web technologies, Software, Mobile-web, Gaming and e-Commerce

3.5%

founderinstitute.com

### DojoBoost
**France,    Paris**

Web technologies, Software, Mobile-web, Gaming and e-Commerce

dojoboost.com

### GameFounders
**Estonia, Tallinn**

Web technologies, Software, Mobile-web, Gaming and e-Commerce

€15000 | 9%

jolt.marsdd.com

### Founder Institute
**Germany**

Web technologies, Software, Mobile-web, Gaming and e-Commerce

3.5%

founderinstitute.com

### Seedcamp
**Germany, Berlin**

Web technologies, Software, Mobile-web, Gaming and e-Commerce

$50,000 | 5-8%

seedcamp.com

### HackFwd
**Germany, Hamburg**

Web technologies, Software, Mobile-web, Gaming and e-Commerce

27%

wayra.org/en

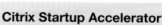

### StartupReykjavik
**Iceland, Reykjavík**

Web technologies, Software, Mobile-web, Gaming and e-Commerce

$16,000 and option $50,000 convertible | 6%

Startupreykjavik.com

### Citrix Startup Accelerator
**India**

Web technologies, Software

$20,000 - $400,000

citrixStartupaccelerator.com

### The Hatch
**India, Chandigarh**

Everything

INR10 lacs - INR 100 lacs

the-hatch.com

### TLabs
**India, Delhi**

Web technologies, Software, Mobile-web, Gaming and e-Commerce

10 LAKS | 10%

tlabs.in

**Le Camping**
**France, Paris**
Web technologies, Software, Mobile-
web, Gaming and e-Commerce
€4,500
lecamping.org

**Wayra**
**German**
Web technologies, Software, Mobile-
web, Gaming and e-Commerce
$30,000 - 70,000 | 10%
wayra.org/en

**Startup Bootcamp**
**Germany, Berlin**
Web technologies, Software, Mobile-
web, Gaming and e-Commerce
€15,000 | 8%
Startupbootcamp.org

**Rocket Internet**
**Germany, Berlin**
Web technologies, Software, Mobile-web,
Gaming and e-Commerce, Retail
rocket-internet.de

**Openfund**
**Greece, Athens**
Web technologies, Software, Mobile-web,
Gaming and e-Commerce
€50,000 | 10%
theopenfund.com

**CoLabs**
**Hungary, Budapest**
Web technologies, Software, Mobile-
web, Gaming and e-Commerce
HUF 2-6M | 10-20%
colabs.hu

**The Morpheus**
**India**
Web technologies, Software, Mobile-
web, Gaming and e-Commerce
5 L INR | 6-9%
themorpheus.com

**iAccelerator**
**India, Bangalore**
Web technologies, Software, Mobile-
web, Gaming and e-Commerce
Rs. 5-10 Lacs
iaccelerator.org

**Venture nursery**
**India, Mumbai**
Web technologies, Software, Mobile-
web, Gaming and e-Commerce
venturenursery.com

**Lightspeed Venture
Partners**
**India, New Delhi**
Consumer, enterprise technology and cleantech
lsvp.com

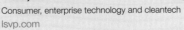

## Wayra
**Ireland**
Web technologies, Software, Mobile-web, Gaming and e-Commerce
$30,000 - 70,000 | 10%
wayra.org/en

## NDRC Launchpad
**Ireland, Dublin**
Web technologies, Software, Mobile-web, Gaming and e-Commerce
ndrc.ie/launchpad

## Startup Bootcamp
**Israel, Haifa**
Web technologies, Software, Mobile-web, Gaming and e-Commerce
€15,000 | 8%
Startupbootcamp.org

## Plarium Labs
**Israel, Hertzeliya**
Gaming
$18,000 | 15%
plariumlabs.com

## Dreamit Ventures
**Israel, Mercaz**
Web technologies, Software, Mobile-web, Gaming and e-Commerce
$25,000 | 6%
dreamitventures.com

## Venturegeeks
**Israel, Petah-Tikva**
Web technologies, Software, Mobile-web, Gaming and e-Commerce
5,000 per founder | 10%
venturegeeks.org

## Oasis 500
**Jordan, Amman**
Digital media and Mobile-web
JD 22,000
oasis500.com

## Savannah Fund
**Kenya**
Web and Mobile
$25,000 - 50,0000
savannah.vc

## Seeqnce
**Lebanon - Beirut**
Web and Mobile
$75,000 | 30% with 10% buyback option
seeqnce.com/index.php

## StartupHighway
**Lithuania, Vilnius**
Web technologies, Software, Mobile-web, Gaming and e-Commerce
€14,000 | 7%
Startuphighway.com

### Propeller Venture Accelerator
**Ireland, Dublin**

Information and Communication Technology

dcu.ie/ryanacademy/propeller.shtml

### Startup Bootcamp
**Ireland, Dublin**

Web technologies, Software, Mobile-web, Gaming and e-Commerce

€15,000 | 8%

Startupbootcamp.org

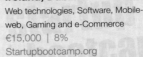

### Microsoft Accelerator
**Israel, Herzliya**

Web technologies, Software, Mobile-web, Gaming and e-Commerce

$20,000 | 6%

microsoft.com/bizspark/
accelerator/azure

### Lightspeed Venture Partners
**Israel, Herzliya Pituach**

Consumer, enterprise technology and cleantech

lsvp.com

### H-Farm
**Italy, Treviso**

Web technologies, Software, Mobile-web, Gaming and e-Commerce

€15,000

h-farmventures.com

### Open Network Lab
**Japan, Tokyo**

Web technologies, Software, Mobile-web, Gaming and e-Commerce

5%

onlab.jp

### 88mph
**Kenya - Nairobi**

Mobile-web

Up to $100,000

88mph.ac

### SK Planet
**Korea, Seoul**

Content Delivery, New Media, Communication & SNS, Commerce, LBS

$20,000 | 6%

skplanet.com/eng

### Wayra
**Mexico**

Web technologies, Software, Mobile-web, Gaming and e-Commerce

$30,000-70,000 | 10%

wayra.org/en

### Founder Institute
**Netherlands**

Web technologies, Software, Mobile-web, Gaming and e-Commerce

3,5%

founderinstitute.com

### VentureSpace Accelerator
**Netherlands, Amsterdam**
Web technologies, Software, Mobile-web,
Gaming and e-Commerce
$20,000
venturespace.nl

### Rockstart
**Netherlands, Amsterdam**
Web technologies, Software, Mobile-web, Gaming and e-Commerce
€15,000 | 8%
rockstart.com

### Venturez
**NL / Worldwide**
Web technologies, Software, Mobile-web, Gaming and e-Commerce
€10,000 - €50,000
venturez.com

### LightningLab
**New Zeland, Wellington**
Web technologies, Software, Mobile-web, Gaming and e-Commerce
NZ$ 18,000
lightninglab.co.nz

### HugeThing
**Poland, Poznan**
Web technologies, Software, Mobile-web, Gaming and e-Commerce
30,000 PLN | 10%
hugething.org

### GammaRebels
**Poland, Warsaw**
Web technologies, Software, Mobile-web, Gaming and e-Commerce
€12,000 | 10%
gammarebels.com

### TexDrive
**Russia, Moscow**
Web technologies, Software, Mobile-web, Gaming and e-Commerce
$26,000 convertible $50,000 | 10%
texdrive.com/eng

### Yandex Factory
**Russia, Moscow**
Web technologies, Software, Mobile-web, Gaming and e-Commerce
company.yandex.com/special_projects/yandex_factory.xml

### Founder Institute
**South Africa**
Web technologies, Software, Mobile-web, Gaming and e-Commerce
3.5%
founderinstitute.com
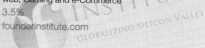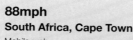

### 88mph
**South Africa, Cape Town**
Mobile-web
Up to $100,000 | 8%
88mph.ac

**Startup Bootcamp**
**Netherlands, Amsterdam**
Web technologies, Software, Mobile-
web, Gaming and e-Commerce
€15,000 | 8%
Startupbootcamp.org

**Dnamo**
**Netherlands, Rotterdam**
Web technologies, Software, Mobile-web,
Gaming and e-Commerce
dnamo.nl

**betaFactory**
**Norway, Oslo**
Web technologies, Software,
Mobile-web, Gaming and e-Commerce
100 kNOK
betafactory.com

**Wayra**
**Peru**
Web technologies, Software, Mobile-
web, Gaming and e-Commerce
$30,000 - 70,000 | 10%
wayra.org/en

**Seed Capital**
**Portugal**
Web technologies, Software, Mobile-
web, Gaming and e-Commerce
$15,000 | 30%
seedcapital.pt

**Seedmoney**
**Romania, Bucharest**
Web technologies, Software, Mobile-
web, Gaming and e-Commerce
€10,000-50,000 | up to 20%
seedmoney.ro

**Joyful Frog Digital
Incubator (JFDI)**
**Singapore**
Web technologies, Software, Mobile-
web, Gaming and e-Commerce
S$25,000 | 6%
jfdi.asia

**Pollenizer**
**Singapore**
Web technologies, Software, Mobile-web,
Gaming and e-Commerce
pollenizer.com

**SparkLabs**
**South Korea, Seoul**
Web technologies, Software, Mobile-web,
Gaming, Digital Media, and e-Commerce
$25,000
sparklabs.co.kr

**Seedcamp**
**Spain**
Web technologies, Software, Mobile-
web, Gaming and e-Commerce
$50,000 | 5-8%
seedcamp.com

### Startup Bootcamp
**Spain**
Web technologies, Software, Mobile-web, Gaming and e-Commerce
€15,000 | 8%
Startupbootcamp.org

### Tetuan Valley
**Spain**
Web technologies, Software, Mobile-web, Gaming and e-Commerce
tetuanvalley.com

### Digital Assets Deployment
**Spain, Madrid**
Web technologies, Software, Mobile-web, Gaming and e-Commerce
€ 50,000-250,000 | 10%
dad.es

### appWorks Ventures Incubator Program
**Taiwan**
Mobile-web
NT $50 million to NT $30 million | 5-20%
appworks.tw/incubator

### Wayra
**United Kingdom**
Web technologies, Software, Mobile-web, Gaming and e-Commerce
£30,000-70,000 | 10%
wayra.org/en

### Citrix Startup Accelerator
**United Kingdom**
Web technologies, Software
£20,000-400,000
citrixStartupaccelerator.com

### Bethnal Green Ventures
**United Kingdom, London**
Web technologies, Software, Mobile-web, Gaming and e-Commerce
£15,000 | 5%
bethnalgreenventures.com

### Pearson Catalyst
**United Kingdom, London**
Education
£10,000 | 5-8%
pearson.com/news/2013/february/introducing-pearson-catalyst--the-edtech-incubator-programme-for.html

### Startup Bootcamp
**United Kingdom, London**
Healthcare
€15,000 | 8%
Startupbootcamp.org

### The Bakery
**United Kingdom, London**
Web technologies, Software, Mobile-web, Gaming and e-Commerce
Up to £50,000 | 2-8%
thebakerylondon.com

## Wayra
**Spain**
Web technologies, Software, Mobile-web, Gaming and e-Commerce
$30,000-70,000 | 10%
wayra.org/en

## SeedRocket
**Spain, Barcelona**
Web technologies, Software, Mobile-web, Gaming and e-Commerce
seedrocket.com

## SeedStartup
**United Arab Emirates, Dubai**
Web technologies, Software, Mobile-web, Gaming and e-Commerce
20,000-25,000 | 10%
seedStartup.com

## University of Surrey 100 Club
**UK, Surrey**
Web technologies, Software, Mobile-web, Gaming and e-Commerce, Retail
surrey.ac.uk/100club

## Accelerator Academy
**United Kingdom, London**
Web technologies, Software, Mobile-web, Gaming and e-Commerce
3-5%
acceleratoracademy.com

**United Kingdom, Birmingham**
Web technologies, Software, Mobile-web, Gaming and e-Commerce

Oxygen Accelerator is a tech accelerator. A 13-week intensive mentor led bootcamp, followed by 13-weeks of incubation that culminates with a series of investor days where you pitch to a large, carefully selected group of Angel investors, VCs and Private Equity groups for next stage funding.

£6,000 per founder | 8%

oxygenaccelerator.com

## Springboard
**United Kingdom, Oxford**
Web technologies, Software, Mobile-web, Gaming and e-Commerce
£5,000 per founder | 6%
wayra.org/en

## Techstars London (formerly Springboard)
**United Kingdom, London**
Web technologies, Software, Mobile-web, Gaming and e-Commerce
€15,000 | 6% + optional €70,000 convertible debt
techstars.com/london

## Seedcamp
**United Kingdom, London**
Web technologies, Software, Mobile-web, Gaming and e-Commerce
£50,000 | 5-8%
seedcamp.com

### Dotforge Accelerator
**United Kingdom, Sheffield**
Web technologies, Software, Mobile-web, Gaming and e-Commerce
£25,000 | 6%
dotforgeaccelerator.com

### White Bear Yard
**United Kingdom, London**
Web technologies, Software, Mobile-web, Gaming and e-Commerce
£10,000 - 250,000
whitebearyard.com

### Beta Foundry
**United Kingdom, Oxford**
Web technologies, Software, Mobile-web, Gaming and e-Commerce
£5,000 | 5-10%
betafoundry.com

### Emerge Education
**United Kingdom, London**
Education Technology
£15,000 | 3-8%
emerge.education

### The Awesome Inc. Experience
**United States**
Web technologies, Software, Mobile-web, Gaming and e-Commerce
$20,000 | 5-6%
awesomeinc.org/the-awesome-experience

### The Founder Institute
**United States**
Web technologies, Software, Mobile-web, Gaming and e-Commerce
Tuition | 3.5%
founderinstitute.com

### Incubate Miami
**United States, Miami**
Web technologies, Software, Mobile-web, Gaming and e-Commerce
$20,000 | 6%
incubatemiami.com

### Flash Point
**United States, Atlanta**
Web technologies, Software, Mobile-web, Gaming and e-Commerce
$25,000 | 8%
flashpoint.gatech.edu

### Accelerate Baltimore
**United States, Baltimore**
Web technologies, Software, Mobile-web, Gaming and e-Commerce
$25,000
acceleratebaltimore.r2ismash.com

### Lester Centre for Entrepreneurship Berkeley
**United States, Berkeley**
Web technologies, Software, Mobile-web, Gaming and e-Commerce
entrepreneurship.berkeley.edu
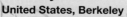

### Searchcamp
**United Kingdom, Middlesbrough**
Web technologies, Software, Mobile-web,
Gaming and e-Commerce
$23,000 | 8%
searchcamp.co

### Ignite100
**United Kingdom, Newcastle**
Web technologies, Software, Mobile-web,
Gaming and e-Commerce
£5,000 per founder | 8%
ignite100.com

### PayPal Startup Accelerator
**United States**
Web technologies, Software, Mobile-web,
Gaming and e-Commerce
Currently on hold
x.com/community/ppx/xspaces/
accelerator

### TechRanch Austin
**United States**
Web technologies, Software, Mobile-
web, Gaming and e-Commerce
techranchaustin.com

### The Start Project
**United States**
Web technologies, Software, Mobile-
web, Gaming and e-Commerce
Tuition $10,000-12,000 | 5-8%
thestartproject.com

### TimeSpace New York Times
**United States**
Publishing
nytimes.com/timespace

### Shotput Ventures
**United States, Atlanta**
Capital Light Web and Mobile
$12,000-18,000 | 5-10%
shotputventures.com

### Capital Factory
**United States, Austin**
Web technologies, Software, Mobile-
web, Gaming and e-Commerce
$20,000 | 5%
capitalfactory.com

### The Unreasonable Institute
**United States, Boulder**
Web technologies, Software, Mobile-web,
Gaming and e-Commerce
unreasonableinstitute.org

### Techstars
**Boulder, Seattle, Chicago, New York,
Austin, Boston, London**
Web technologies, Software, Mobile-web, Gaming and
e-Commerce
$18,000 | 6% + optional $100,00 convertible debt
Techstars.com
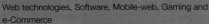

ACCELERATE

**Brooklyn Beta
Summer Camp**
**United States, Brooklyn**
Web technologies, Software, Mobile-web,
Gaming and e-Commerce
brooklynbeta.org/summer-camp

**Summer @ Highland**
**United States - Cambridge
and Menlo Park**
Web technologies, Software, Mobile-web,
Gaming and e-Commerce
$16,000
summer.hcp.comaccelerator

**Co.Lab accerator**
**United States, Chattanooga**
Web technologies, Software, Mobile-web,
Gaming and e-Commerce
colab.is

**ImpactEngine**
**United States, Chicago**
Tech Solutions to societal,
environmental, clean water and
sustainable employment challenges
$20,000 | 7%
theimpactengine.com

**Innov8 for Health**
**United States, Cincinatti**
Health
innov8forhealth.com

**Brandery**
**United States, Cincinnati**
Web technologies, Software, Mobile-
web, Gaming and e-Commerce
$20,000 | 6%
brandery.org

**LaunchHouse**
**United States, Cleveland**
Web technologies, Software, Mobile-web,
Gaming and e-Commerce
launchhouse.com

**10-xcelerator**
**United States, Columbus**
Web technologies
$20,000 | 6%
10xelerator.com

**The Ark**
**United States, Fayetteville, AR**
Web technologies, Software, Mobile-web,
Gaming and e-Commerce
$20,000 | 6%
arkchallenge.org

**Start Garden**
**United States, Grand Rapids**
Everything
$5000 And follow on funding up to
$500,000
startgarden.com

### iVentures10
**United States - Champaign**

Web technologies, Software, Mobile-web, Gaming and e-Commerce

£5,000 per founder

iventures10.com

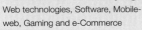

---

### Healthbox
**United States - Chicago and Boston**

Healthcare

$50,000 | 7%

healthbox.com

---

### Bizdom U
**United States, Cleveland**

Web technologies, Software, Mobile-web, Gaming and e-Commerce

$25,000 | 8%

bizdom.com

---

### Tech Wildcatter
**United States, Dallas**

B2B and B2B2C technologies

$25,000 | 7-10%

techwildcatters.com

---

### The Iron Yard
**United States - Greenville and Spartanburg, SC**

Web technologies, Software, Mobile-web, Gaming and e-Commerce

$20,000 | 6%

www.theironyard.com

---

### Techstars Chicago (formerly Excelerate Labs)
**United States, Chicago**

Web technologies, Software, Mobile-web, Gaming and e-Commerce

$25,000 - 50,000 | 6%

exceleratelabs.com

---

### Flashstarts
**United States, Cleveland**

Web technologies, Software, Mobile-web, Gaming and e-Commerce

$20,000 | 6%

flashstarts.com

---

### DUhatch (Duke University)
**United States, Durham**

Web technologies, Software, Mobile-web, Gaming and e-Commerce

cerc.duke.edu/duhatch

---

### Blue Startups
**United States, Honolulu**

Web technologies, Software, Mobile-web, Gaming and e-Commerce

$20,000 | 6%

blueStartups.com

### XLR8HI
**United States, Honolulu**
Sciences and Tourism
$50,000
xlr8hi.com

### Houston Tech Center
**United States, Houston**
Web technologies, Software, Mobile-web, Gaming and e-Commerce
houstontech.org

### NMotion
**United States, Lincoln**
Financial services, healthcare, manufacturing, transportation/logistics, communications, and agriculture
$15,000 | 6%
nmotion.co

### Amplify.LA
**United States, Los Angeles**
Web technologies, Software, Mobile-web, Gaming and e-Commerce
$50,000-150,000 | 5-15%
amplify.la/accelerator

### StartEngine
**United States, Los Angeles**
Web technologies, Software, Mobile-web, Gaming and e-Commerce
$20,000 | 10%
startengine.com

### Media Camp
**United States, Los Angeles, San Francisco**
Media
$20,000
mediacamp.com

### ZeroTo510
**United States, Memphis**
Medical Devices
$50,000 | 15%
zeroto510.com/index.html

### Upstart Memphis
**United States - Memphis, Texas**
Women led -Web technologies, Software, Mobile-web, Gaming and e-Commerce
$15,000 | 6%
upstartmemphis.com

### gener8tor
**United States, Milwaukee**
Web technologies, Software, Mobile-web, Gaming and e-Commerce
$20,000 | 6-9%
gener8tor.com
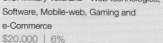

### Victory Spark
**United States, Milwaukee**
U.S. Military Veterans - Web technologies, Software, Mobile-web, Gaming and e-Commerce
$20,000 | 6%
victoryspark.com

## SURGE Accelerator
**United States, Houston**
Energy Software
$30,000 w/ convertible of $50,000 | 6%
surgeaccelerator.com/home

## Sproutbox
**United States, Indiana**
Web technologies and Subscription
Based Models
$10,000 - $20,000 | 20-40%
sproutbox.com

## K5Launch
**United States, Los Angeles**
Web technologies, Software, Mobile-
web, Gaming and e-Commerce
Up to $25,000 | 6-8%
k5launch.com

## LaunchPadLA
**United States, Los Angeles**
Web technologies, Software, Mobile-web,
Gaming and e-Commerce
$50,000 | 6%
launchpad.la

## XLerateHealth
**United States, Louisville**
Health
$20,000 | 6%
xleratehealth.com/

## Seed Hatchery
**United States, Memphis**
Web technologies, Software, Mobile-web,
Gaming and e-Commerce
$15,000 | 6%
seedhatchery.com

## Launch Pad Tech
**United States, Miami**
Tech Solutions for Hospitality, Tourism,
Healthcare, Creatives (art, design, music,
photography, etc.)
$25,000
venturehive.co

## SPARK Accelerator
**United States, Michigan**
Web technologies, Software, Mobile-
web, Gaming and e-Commerce
$25,000
annarborusa.org/start-ups/spark-
business-accelerator

## Project Skyway
**United States, Minneapolis**
Web and Mobile
$6,000 | 9%
projectskyway.com/about

## 500 Startups
**United States, Mountain View**
Web technologies, Software, Mobile-
web, Gaming and e-Commerce
$50,000 | 5%
500.co

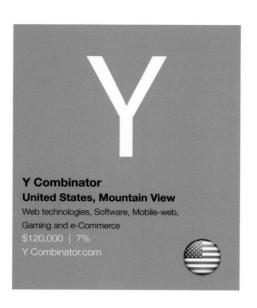

### Y Combinator
**United States, Mountain View**
Web technologies, Software, Mobile-web,
Gaming and e-Commerce
$120,000 | 7%
Y Combinator.com

### JumpStart Foundry
**United States, Nashville**
Web technologies, Software, Mobile-
web, Gaming and e-Commerce
$15,000 | 10%
jumpstartfoundry.com

### New York Digital Health Accelerator
**United States, New York**
Healthcare
$100,000
digitalhealthaccelerator.com

### Startl
**United States, New York**
Education Technology
startl.org/

### Women Innovate Mobile
**United States, New York**
Web technologies, Software, Mobile-web,
Gaming and e-Commerce
$18,000 | 6%
wim.co

### The Hatchery
**United States, Northern California**
Web technologies, Software, Mobile-web,
Gaming and e-Commerce
hatchery.vc

### UpTech
**United States - Northern Kentucky, Cincinnati**
Web and Mobile
9%
uptechideas.org

### Dreamit Ventures
**United States - Philadephia, New York, Austin**
Web technologies, Software, Mobile-
web, Gaming and e-Commerce
$25,000 | 6%
dreamitventures.com

### Edson Student Entrepreneur
**United States, Phoenix**
Web technologies, Software, Mobile-web,
Gaming and e-Commerce
$20,000
studentventures.asu.edu/about

**Blueprint Health**
**United States, New York**
Healthcare
$20,000 | 6%
blueprinthealth.org

**Kaplan edTech**
**United States, New York**
Education
$20,000 | 6%
kaplanedtechaccelerator.com

**NYC SeedStart**
**United States, New York**
Web technologies, Software, Mobile-web,
Gaming and e-Commerce
$20,000 | 5%
nycseedstart.com

**Socratic Labs**
**United States, New York**
Education Technology
$20,000 - 25,000
socraticlabs.com/Welcome.html

**Hatch**
**United States, Norfolk**
Web technologies, Software, Mobile-
web, Gaming and e-Commerce
$25,000 | 8%
hatchnorfolk.com

**triangleStartupfactory**
**United States, North Carolina**
Web technologies, Software, Mobile-
web, Gaming and e-Commerce
$50,000 | 7.5%
triangleStartupfactory.com

**The NYU-Poly DUMBO Incubator**
**United States - NYC**
poly.edu/business/incubators/
dumbo

**OCTANe LaunchPad**
**United States, Orange County**
Web technologies, Software, Mobile-web,
Gaming and e-Commerce
octaneoc.org
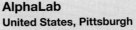

**Entrepreneurs Roundtable Accelerator**
**United States, New York**
Web technologies, Software, Mobile-web,
Gaming and e-Commerce
$40,000 | 8%
eranyc.com

**AlphaLab**
**United States, Pittsburgh**
Web technologies, Software, Mobile-
web, Gaming and e-Commerce
$25,000 | 3%
alphalab.org

### NIKE + ACCELERATOR
**United States, Portland**
Sport software, Mobile-web
$20,000 | 6%
nikeaccelerator.com

### Portland Incubator Experiment (PIE)
**United States, Portland**
Web technologies, Software, Mobile-web,
Gaming and e-Commerce
$20,000
piepdx.com

### Betaspring
**United States, Rhode Island**
Web technologies, Software, Mobile-web,
Gaming and e-Commerce
$20,000 | 6-10%
betaspring.com

### AngelPad
**United States, San Francisco**
Web technologies, Software, Mobile-web, Gaming and e-Commerce
$20,000 | 6%
angelpad.org

### Kicklabs
**United States, San Francisco**
Web technologies, Software, Mobile-web, Gaming and e-Commerce
kicklabs.com

### Matter
**United States, San Francisco**
Media
$50,000
matter.vc

### Citrix Startup Accelerator
**United States, Santa Clara**
Web technologies, Software
$20,000 - 400,000
citrixStartupaccelerator.com

### InnoSpring
**United States, Santa Clara**
Web technologies, Software, Mobile-web, Gaming and e-Commerce
$50,000 - 100,000
innospring.net

### Founders Co-op
**United States, Seattle**
Web technologies, Software, Mobile-web, Gaming and e-Commerce
$50,000 - 250,000
founderscoop.com

### Microsoft Accelerator
**United States, Seattle**
Web technologies, Software, Mobile-web, Gaming and e-Commerce
$20,000 | 6%
microsoft.com/BizSpark/accelerator

**Portland Seed Fund**
**United States, Portland**
Education Technology
$25,000
portlandseedfund.com

**The Portland Ten**
**United States, Portland and Seattle**
Web technologies, Software, Mobile-web, Gaming and e-Commerce
portlandten.com

**Code for America Accelerator**
**United States, San Francisco**
Web technologies, Software, Mobile-web, Gaming and e-Commerce
$25,000 | Not specified
codeforamerica.org/accelerator

**Hub Ventures**
**United States, San Francisco**
Web technologies, Software, Mobile-web, Gaming and e-Commerce
$20,000 | 6%
hub-ventures.com

**Pearson Catalyst**
**United States, San Francisco**
Education
$10,000
pearson.com/news/2013/february/
introducing-pearson-catalyst--the-
edtech-incubator-programme-for.html

**RockHealth**
**United States, San Francisco**
Healthcare
$100K convertible note
rockhealth.com/about

**Mucker Lab**
**United States, Santa Monica**
Web technologies, Software, Mobile-web, Gaming and e-Commerce
$21,000 | 6-8%
muckerlab.com

**Arizona Furnace**
**United States, Scottsdale**
Web technologies, Software, Mobile-web, Gaming and e-Commerce
azfurnace.org

**Boost VC**
**United States, Silicon Valley**
Web technologies, Software, Mobile-web, Crypto Currency, Gaming and e-Commerce
$10,000-15,000 | 5%
boost.vc

**HAXLR8R**
**United States, Silicon Valley**
Hardware
$25,000 | 8%
haxlr8r.com

### MindTheBridge
**United States, Silicon Valley**

Disruptive technologies in mobile, big data, digital publishing, educational platforms, design, fashion and online payment

Up to $65,000 | 9%

seedquest.mindthebridge.org

### Plug and Play Startup Camp
**United States, Silicon Valley**

Web technologies, Software, Mobile-web, Gaming and e-Commerce

$25,000

plugandplayStartupcamp.com

### The Alchemist Accelerator
**United States, Silicon Valley**

Enterprise

$28,000 | 4%

alchemistaccelerator.com

### Capital Innovators
**United States, St. Louis**

Web technologies, Software, Mobile-web, Gaming and e-Commerce

$50,000 | 5-10%

capitalinnovators.com

### Telluride Venture Accelerator
**United States - Telluride, CO**

Outdoor Recreation, Tourism, Natural Products, Health, Energy, Water, and Education.

$30,000 | 4%

tellurideva.com

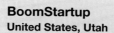

### BoomStartup
**United States, Utah**

Web technologies, Software, Mobile-web, Gaming and e-Commerce

$20,000 | 6%

boomStartup.com

### Fortify Ventures
**United States, Washington**

Web technologies, Software, Mobile-web, Gaming and e-Commerce

$25,000

fortifyventures.com

### Lightspeed Venture Partners
**United States, Silicon Valley**

Consumer, enterprise technology and cleantech

lsvp.com

### Tandem
**United States, Silicon Valley**

Mobile

$200,000 | 10%

tandemcap.com/index.html

### Upwest Labs
**United States, Silicon Valley**

Web technologies, Software, Mobile-web, Gaming and e-Commerce

$20,000 | 8%

upwestlabs.com

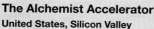

### Lean Launch Ventures
**United States, Stamford**

Web technologies, Software, Mobile-web, Gaming and e-Commerce

$20,000 - 25,000 | 6%

llventures.co

### StartFast Venture Accelerator
**United States, Syracuse**

Web technologies, Software, and Mobile-web

$18,000 | 6%

startfast.net

### Startup Utah
**United States, Utah**

Web technologies, Software, Mobile-web, Gaming and e-Commerce

Startuputah.com

### Acceleprise
**United States, Washington**

Web technologies, Software, Mobile-web, Gaming and e-Commerce

$30,000 | 5%

acceleprise.vc

### Imagine K12
**United States, Silicon Valley**

Education

$14,000 - 20,000 | 2-10%

imaginek12.com

### Wayra
**Venezuela**

Web technologies, Software, Mobile-web, Gaming and e-Commerce

$30,000-70,000 | 10%

wayra.org/en

FIN

THOU

AL

GHTS

# FINAL
# THOUGHTS

It's tempting to want to take everything these entrepreneurs have told us and cram together a definitive list of do's and don't's, when-to-do's and when to don't's, how-to-do's and how-to-don't's. But doing that would be playing a massive trick on you—leaving you to believe that anyone has a clue of what YOU need to do as a founder, or what YOUR startup needs. What you've read is a surplus of advice from founders who know what has worked and hasn't worked for them. While some insights are very widely applicable, there are some that relate strongly and only to startups, and founders in particular industries, stages, and locations. Take from it what you need.

Though there is no substitute for reading through Accelerate's compendium of founders' thoughts, the broad and overarching themes of advice that deserve honorable mention for having been most frequently and deservedly prescribed can be found below:

**Do Stuff:** If you haven't acted at least twice as much as you've talked, then there is something wrong.

**User Acquisition:** It starts here and it ends here. Most else depends on it.

**Focus:** Know what is a waste of time and what is most important. In other words, separate the ice cream from the horseshit; the ice cream does nothing for the horseshit, but the horseshit ruins the taste of the ice cream.

**Accelerators:** In 1959 there was one incubator: Batavia Industrial Center in New York. In 2005 there was one accelerator: Y Combinator. Now, in 2013, there are hundreds. This trend tells us that accelerator programs are growing in popularity just as startups are. With big numbers come nuances, and with nuances, it pays to know what you're getting into. That said, keep in mind some of the more important elements of joining an accelerator.

**Teams:** Accelerators pick teams, not individuals, not necessarily ideas and not your pitch. Your team is the linchpin of it all—it ties all that other good stuff together.

**Accelerator-Startup Fit:** You need to figure out what is most important to your startup, who you need to know, what you need to know, and which accelerator can get you that. Be sure to know the type of founders, industry experts, and influencers you need to know to move your company in the right direction. If the network or community you need to bring your product to market isn't there, then it isn't there and maybe you shouldn't be either. Fundraising, which I'm mentioning last, is of course a factor, but judging from what the 150 founders explained to us about getting into an accelerator, it shouldn't be of the highest priority. The money you'll get out of an accelerator experience is one form of currency, yes, but the various other forms such as mentorship, exposure, and introductions have far greater multiplier effects than the linear nature of money.

---

We are honored that *Accelerate* has been able to feature such a tremendous mix of founders with a breadth of experience, industry focus, and practical insight. Without them, it would not have been possible to create this book. We also could not, and would not, have done this without your curiosity and pursuit of entrepreneurship.

We would be committing blasphemy if we marketed, financed, and authored a book prescribing—among many things—user insight and feedback without practicing it ourselves. With that said, we would love to hear your thoughts on the book including what we did well and what we did poorly. Please send your thoughts to accelerate@fgpress.com or post a review where you purchased the book.

# THANK YOU FOR READING!

# RECOMMENDED
# READING

### *Running Lean*

Ash Maurya

O'Reilly Media , 2012

### *Venture Deals*

Brad Feld & Jason Mendelson

John Wiley & Sons, 2011

### *The Entrepreneur Equation*

Carol Roth

BenBella Books, 2012

### *Angel Investing*

David S. Rose

Wiley, 2014

## The Lean Startup

Eric Ries

Crown Business, 2011

## The 4 Steps to the Epiphany

Steven Blank

Lulu Enterprises Incorporated, 2003

## The Start Up Owner's Manual

Steve Blank

K&S Ranch -Publishing, 2012

## Blue Ocean Strategy

W. Chan Kim and Renée Mauborgne

Harvard Business School Press, 2005

# ABOUT THE AUTHORS

**Luke Deering** is Co-founder and CEO at VineUp. Prior to VineUp, Luke worked for Estée Lauder before joining New York City startup Panjiva, shortly after it raised $5m in venture capital funding.

Luke is an avid basketball player, winning the Under 20's British National Basketball Championship in 2001, while attending the National Sports academy in Durham England. Luke's passion for basketball was the catalyst for his move from the UK to the US.

After suffering an injury and returning to the UK, Luke turned his efforts from basketball to academia and made a second move to the US. Upon returning, he attended several colleges before settling at Montclair State University on a full academic scholarship. Despite struggling with dyslexia, Luke went on to become Academic All-American and was presented with several other awards including The Wall-Street Journal Award for Outstanding Academic Achievement.

Luke holds a degree in Economics.

**Matt Cartagena** is VP of Marketing for VineUp, co-creator of Howtowritea-businessplan.com, and Online Marketing Consultant. Matt has worked as an analyst for UPS, Stryker Corporation, and Party City before shifting gears towards the exciting world of startups.

Despite his complicated relationship with academics, Matt went on to become 1 of 6 graduating students recognized for Outstanding Achievement and the recipient of Becker Professional Education's CPA scholarship.

Matt enjoys Crossfit, traveling cheaply, and reading non-fiction. Matt also holds a degree in Economics and an MBA from Montclair State University.

**Chris Dowdeswell** is Co-founder and CTO at VineUp. Chris has been involved in developing web applications for 15 years and has worked on a variety of projects for blue chips including Peugeot, Madame Tussauds and AXA insurance.

Chris was also part of the team that created "InControl", a web system to track infectious disease in NHS hospitals.

One of Chris's more notable projects was developing the Learning Resource Kit, which was created to help evaluate spending in secondary schools across the United Kingdom. The LRK was launched in the houses of parliament by the then Secretary for Education (now Home Secretary) Theresa May, and has since been used by more than 16,000 schools.

In his spare time, Chris enjoys mountain biking and relaxing with his two young daughters Ettie and Daisy.